Chocolates By Imagination

Spring and Summer

Daisy Favors page 38

Second Edition

Chocolates By Imagination

Spring and Summer

Sonia Nance

TATE PUBLISHING
AND ENTERPRISES, LLC

Published by Tate Publishing & Enterprises, LLC
127 E. Trade Center Terrace | Mustang, Oklahoma 73064 USA
1.888.361.9473 | www.tatepublishing.com

Tate Publishing is committed to excellence in the publishing industry. The company reflects the philosophy established by the founders, based on Psalm 68:11,
"The Lord gave the word and great was the company of those who published it."

Book design copyright © 2014 by Tate Publishing, LLC. All rights reserved.

Published in the United States of America
ISBN: 978-1-63185-557-3
1. Cooking/Courses & Dishes/Chocolate
2. Cooking Entertaining
14.03.14

Sonia Nance
Chocolates By Imagination: Spring and Summer. Adorable and Delicious Molded and Dipped Confections you can make at home/by Sonia Nance

Confection and Food styling by Chocolates By Imagination.

Front Cover - Sunflower Favors, page 47
Back Cover - Dipped Strawberries, page 150

Printed in The United States of America

Visit our website at www.chocolatesbyimagination.com

Special Thanks

Jim Reeve who continuously pours out his heart and in doing so caused my heart to heal and grow.

Dawn Jackson who taught me character is built in those unseen places.

Grace Wabuke who showed me excellence is obtainable and well worth the price.

Kelly DuPee who led me passed fear and into trust.

Milk Chocolate Coatings

Acknowledgments

Among the many I wish to thank are;

Teresa Falicon who stuck with me through the pretty and the ugly. It was a joy to have you around all those years. Thank you for your unwavering dedication and friendship.

Eric Cheng's patience and beautiful photography turned a simple cookbook into a work of art.

Jodi Krone, my good friend, thank you for your precious time and beautiful photography.

My beautiful daughters Erin and Natalie who gave up a lot so Mom could pursue her dream. Thank you for believing in me.

Mom and Dad, you were the first to come along side the dream and you have never given up on me. I could not have made it without you. Thank you will never cover how much I appreciate all you do. I love you.

Contents

Rose Box page 68

Introduction

I want you to forget anything scary you have heard about chocolate making and start fresh here with me. After thirty years of making chocolate flavored confections I can assure you there is nothing complicated, mysterious or threatening about it. We are simply going to melt them, shape them, cool them, eat them or decorate them and give as gifts. It is my highest priority with this book that you are successful in making these wonderful confections. And my hope that you will find as much enjoyment in preparing, sampling and giving these confections as I have.

Thirty years ago I was invited to an in-home chocolate party. I sat quietly through the presentation and demonstrations and decided it did not seem that difficult. I purchased a few items and soon discovered it really is pretty simple. That is once I stopped burning the chocolate coatings. At that time I was working in retail and had fifty employees. I wanted to give Christmas gifts to them, but could not afford to. Luckily, there was a cake and candy store very close to where I worked. She had everything I needed and more. I made cute little bell and tree confections, I put them in a little Christmas box and handed them out at work. You would have thought I had given them the winning lottery ticket. No one could believe I made them and I could not believe the response. I was so happy I could give everyone something and they truly loved it. There was no turning back from there. Eventually my kitchen turned into a confection factory. Family, friends and co-workers started ordering confections for their special occasions and I began selling my confections at local boutiques. In June of 1995, with the help and support of my family, I opened Chocolates By Imagination, my very own manufacturing facility. I have had the incredible opportunity to make confections for company's like Disney, McDonalds, Sam's Club and Costco. And no less important, countless weddings, baby showers and special events for my local customers. I have never taken a formal class for chocolate making, but have spent the last thirty years testing, perfecting and changing the confection making process. It is time I share that with you.

As you go through this book and try different recipes and make the different confections, I hope that I have given you my years of experience, and that making chocolates flavored confections will become a joyful time you can experience with your family and friends.

I recommend you spend some time in the instructions section of this book, especially the melting chocolate coatings section. It will prepare you for years of confection fun.

Now its time to let *your* imagination take over. And remember, there is never enough free confection.

All my best, Sonia

Basics

Compound Coating Buttons: For this book I recommend using chocolate coatings. They are chocolate flavored coatings with the uniform texture and rich color of real chocolate. Cocoa powder and pure vegetable oils are substituted for chocolate liquor and cocoa butter. Also know as confectionery coatings. These are wonderfully prepared buttons that do not need to be tempered. They come in a large variety of colors and flavors and are excellent for molding and dipping anything. They taste great and will help you be successful with all your molding and dipping recipes. Keep them in a cool dry place and they will last up to six months.

Lets talk coatings: Once you have mastered the melting of the chocolate coatings, the sky's the limit. The single most important step in making these beautiful and delicious molded and dipped confections, is properly melting the buttons. Each flavor of chocolate coatings have a characteristic all their own. Therefore I will address each flavor individually.

Dark Chocolate Flavored Coatings are the most forgiving of the four types of coatings I will go over in this book. The Dark chocolate coating buttons that I use are by no means bitter and I highly recommend them for dipping. Dark chocolate coatings have the highest cocoa powder content and hence the most chocolate flavor. They have less fat and sugar than the other coatings mentioned in this book and is the most enjoyable to work with. It also looks the most decadent.

Milk Chocolate Flavored Coatings are the big favorite. They also melt easily and dip well. As the name revels, they have more milk in them compared to the dark coatings and also more sugar. If you are ever in doubt about which flavor of compound coatings to use, milk chocolate coatings are your best bet. Even dark chocolate lovers will try a good milk chocolate confection.

White and Dyed Chocolate Flavored Coatings. There is no actual cocoa in these and is not truly chocolate. Sometimes I refer to it as vanilla. They are the most versatile of the flavors in that you can dye it any color you can imagine and it marries well with the dark and the milk chocolate coatings. Many of my customers prefer it for their kids because it has no caffeine and people with cocoa allergies seem to have no problem with the white chocolate coatings.

That said, They are a little fussy in the melting process, especially if it has coloring in it. Take extra care when melting this one, because of the high sugar content it can burn easier. Low heat is the secret.

Temperature is everything. You never want your chocolate coatings to be hot. We are not going to cook it, we are going to warm it. You should always be able to touch and hold the warming bowls and the chocolate coatings. When using a microwave or a double broiler, low heat levels are key. I have burned several batches of chocolate coatings over the years, so I recommend starting with small amounts until you fill comfortable with your microwave. So you are not surprised, burning chocolate coatings smell like burning marshmallows. So, if your kitchen starts to smell like a camp out, it's too late. Burning chocolate coatings are extremely hot and can burn you. Also, they may put out a lot of smoke. Use the care with burnt chocolate coatings as you would with a hot dish from the oven. I recommend if you do happen to burn a batch, use pot holders to remove the bowl from the microwave and set the bowl out side in a safe place until it cools off and stops smoking. There is no saving the chocolate coatings at this point. All great chocolatiers have burned a batch or two so throw the burnt batch out and start again. Remember, you're in good company.

Water and Chocolate Coatings do not mix. Never use water base food coloring in your chocolate coatings. (The food color we use for cookies and frosting is water base). I use an oil based food color without flavors. You can find these colorings where they sell chocolate supplies and on our website. Be extra careful with double broilers. Even a small amount of stem or water can turn your chocolate coatings to a consistency of rice pudding. Not what we are looking for.

If you live where there is high humidity and your chocolate coatings are thick like peanut butter, you may need to wait for a less humid day or invest in a de-humidifier. I have a de-humidifier in my kitchen and it is very helpful. In any case, water and chocolate coatings do not mix so be good to yourself and stay away from the water.

A few helpful hints:
- Chocolate coatings shrink a little when you melt it.
- Chocolate coatings can be completely melted and you cannot tell until you stir it.
- The aroma and flavor are best when the coatings are melted. (So go ahead and try some).
- Always use microwave safe bowls. It is important that your bowls do not get hot or your chocolate coatings could burn.
- All chocolate coatings will keep melted on a warming tray for many hours.

Saving and Reheating Chocolate Coatings: chocolate coatings: When you have finished with the chocolate coatings, take the spoon and skewer out of the bowl and cover the bowl with plastic wrap. Store in a cool dry place. When you are ready to reuse the chocolate coatings simply melt as recommended on page 20.

Static in the Mold: This is a common problem, one I deal with daily at the factory. It is when the chocolate flavored coatings fly around the mold in places you did not intend for it to go. Static occurs in your molds when the humility is low and when you are using your molds repeatedly. There is an easy solution. Dampen a clean paper`towel. Wipe the entire inside of the mold with the damp paper towel. You will need to repeat this step each time you unmold your coatings and reuse the mold. If you are using multiple molds, simply lay the damp paper towel on the mold until you are ready to use it. If you have a humidifier you can also try raising the humility in your work room. Be careful you do not over do it.

Warming Trays are a part of our everyday operation at Chocolates By Imagination. They are perfect for holding the chocolate coatings at the best temperature for long periods of time. Especially the colored coatings that tend to burn easily. If you would like to try using a warming tray, ask your friends and family if they have one. You might be surprised how many people have one but never use them. If you think you will be using chocolate coatings often I highly recommend a warming tray. Be sure to use the low heat setting.

Some people use a heating pad to keep the chocolate coatings melted. Cover it with plastic and use as you would a warming tray. Start with low heat.

Microwaves are also used daily in our manufacturing process. I give lesson on melting chocolate coatings in the microwave because it is a critical start to the process. The new microwaves run on very high heat so we use 50% and 60% power. Never higher. When we get a new microwave I always take time and run a few batches to insure successful melting and avoid burning. Keep your run times short, 30 to 60 seconds until you are confident with your microwave. Always stir your chocolate coatings in between run times. The microwave is perfect to re-warm coatings if it starts to cool while you're working on a project. Remember to use less heat to re-warm the chocolate coatings since they are already partially melted.

Double Broilers: If you prefer this method keep a few things in mind. It is not necessary to boil your water. Only bring the water to a simmer then remove it from the heat and place the coatings over the water. As mentioned before chocolate coatings and water do not mix. Any amount of steam that gets into the chocolate coatings will spoil the entire batch. This method is fine if you need only one type of chocolate coating as if for dipping and molding plain pieces.

Melting Chocolate Flavored Compound Coatings

Dark Chocolate Flavored Compound Coatings: Place 1 cup or more dark chocolate flavored coating buttons in a microwave safe bowl. Place in microwave. Use 50% power for 40 seconds. Stir coatings. Repeat until you have a creamy smooth chocolate like consistency. You will need to make any necessary adjustments in the warming time depending on your microwave. Set on warming tray to hold until ready to use.

Milk Chocolate Flavored Compound Coatings: Place 1 cup or more milk chocolate flavored coating buttons in a microwave safe bowl. Place in microwave. Use 50% power for 40 seconds. Stir coatings. Repeat until you have a creamy smooth chocolate like consistency. You will need to make any necessary adjustments in the warming time depending on your microwave. Set on warming tray to hold until ready to use.

White Chocolate Flavored Compound Coatings: Place 1 cup or more white chocolate flavored coating buttons in a microwave safe bowl. Place in microwave. Use 50% power for 30 seconds. Stir coatings. Repeat until you have a creamy smooth chocolate like consistency. You will need to make any necessary adjustments in the warming time depending on your microwave. Set on warming tray to hold until ready to use.

White Chocolate Flavored Compound Coating Colors: Place ½ cup or more colored chocolate flavored coating buttons in a microwave safe bowl. Place in microwave. Use 50% power for 30 seconds. Stir coatings. Repeat until you have a creamy smooth chocolate like consistency. You will need to make any necessary adjustments in the warming time depending on your microwave. Set on warming tray to hold until ready to use.

White Chocolate Coatings

Milk Chocolate Coatings

Dark Chocolate Coatings

Techniques

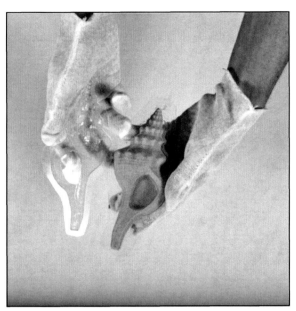

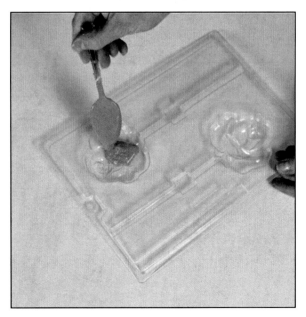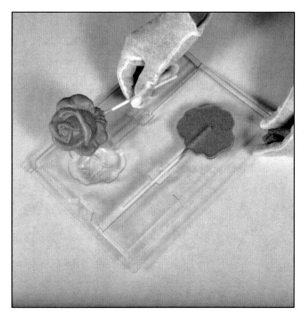

Painting: Now that your chocolate coatings are melted you are ready to make the recipes in this book. Many of the recipes have layers of chocolate coatings. I will use the Tea Pot Favor from page 58 as an example to explain the correct technique. The first layer is the pink flower. The second layer is the green leafs and the third layer is the white chocolate coatings. Each of these layers overlap the other with warm chocolate coatings. Even when you allow the first layer to dry, it can be melted again by the next layer. What is important is to allowed each layer of chocolate coatings to dry completely before you apply the next layer. When the layers have not dried completely they may smear in the mold.

Applying colors to your confections make then fun and unique. In this book I recommend using a medium size wood skewer as your paint brush. The skewer allows you to access small spaces and they are disposable for easy clean up. Simply dip the skewer into the desired color of coatings and apply to your mold just as you would a painting.

Painting with chocolate coatings may also be done after you un-mold the confection. Many times the eyes or other details need to be applied after the confection is out of the mold. Remember let all confections dry completely before serving or packaging.

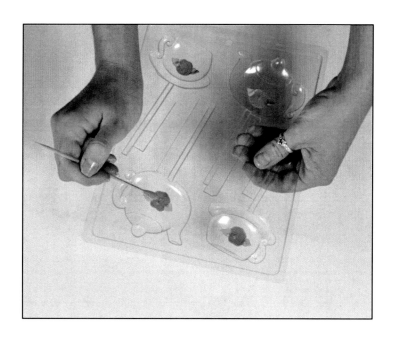

Molding: When filling the mold cavity with chocolate coatings, spoon small amounts of coatings at a time. Fill only the area that will make your particular confection. Do not fill the entire mold area unless instructed to. It can be very messy if the mold cavities become over filled. If this does happen, cool the chocolate coatings in the refrigerator and trim the confection with a paring knife or un-mold as instructed on the following page, then remelt the coatings.

After you fill the mold cavity, tap the mold gently on the counter. This will release air bubbles and smooth out the chocolate coatings.
If called for, this is the time to place the paper stick into the chocolate coatings. The molds have a specific area to place the sticks. Use them as your guide. Place the stick is on the chocolate coatings, push down and roll the stick with your finger so that the top section is covered with coatings. This will provide a studier hold.

Three dimensional molding: Each recipe for 3-D molding has specific instructions pertaining to that item. Please see the recipe.

Cooling: Just as your chocolate coatings do not like to be hot, they also do not like to be too cold. When cooling the chocolate coatings place the mold on a completely flat shelf in the refrigerator and cool for 10 to 30 minutes depending on the thickness of the coatings. The confections will release from the mold easily when they are cooled completely.

If you leave the confections in the refrigerator too long they will become wet and sticky. They are still ok to eat but a little sticky. Let them dry completely before serving or packaging.

To check if the confections are ready, touch them with clean fingers and feel if they are cold. When they feel cold take them out of the refrigerator and un-mold.

Un-Molding: Your confections will release from the molds easily when they are cooled completely. Hold the mold in both hands and gently twist the mold left then right. You may here a little crackling noise. That is the confection releasing from the mold. If the confection is cooled enough it will pop right out. If the confection does not pop right out, put it back in the refrigerator for several more minutes and try again.

There are two ways to remove the confections from the mold.

#1. Holding the mold with your right hand, place your left hand on top of the confections. Holding the mold close to the counter, turn the mold upside down and the confections will fall out. Be careful with this method because the confections will break if they fall on the counter.

#2. For favors, release the confection from the mold using the left to right twist as above. Holding on to the paper stick simply pull the favor from the mold.

Three dimensional confections have special techniques. See the recipe instructions.

Packaging and Decorating: I always put my creations into a cellophane bag. This will keep your beautiful confections fresh and clean. It also makes them easer to stack or use for decorations and hand out at parties. This is a great time to keep that imagination going. The craft stores have a terrific assortment of ribbons and other items to embellish your confection favors and gifts. Packaging can be just as creative as the confections, so I recommend you check out your local craft store or our web site for some new ideas.

Equipment

There are many types of equipment and tools that can be used for making confections. Here, I will go over what is needed for the recipes in this book. You may be surprised that you already have many of these items.

Microwave Oven: Today's microwave oven is very useful in melting chocolate coatings. They have temperature settings that keep the heat low and turn tables built in. Both of these features are ideal for melting chocolate coatings. Choose your bowls for melting coatings carefully. Use only microwave safe bowls. Other bowls may get too hot and burn your coatings. I recommend practicing with a few small batches of coatings until you feel comfortable with the heat setting. See melting chocolate flavored compound coatings in the Basics section on page 20.

Warming Trays: When working with many different colors of chocolate coatings, a warming tray or plate will hold the coatings in a melted state for many hours. Warming trays with temperature controls will allow you to maintain an ideal temperature and avoid burning the chocolate coatings. They will hold many small bowls with your desired colors of coatings like a painters pallet. Some warming trays are too hot for prolonged use with chocolate coatings. If you find you're warming tray is too hot, place a small cooling rack on top of the warming tray. Then place your bowls on top of the cooling rack. Many large department stores carry warming trays or see our website.

Double broilers see page 19.

Tools of the Trade

I have found my favorite chocolate tools and I stick with them. Feel free to try different tools that may work well for you.

Molds come in every size and shape. They are made of clear plastic and are very durable. I've used mine hundreds of times before they need to be replaced. They are easy to care for, simply wash with warm soapy water, rinse completely, and dry with a dust free cloth to remove any water spots. Store them in a box or bag to keep them clean and they will give you many years of use. Like chocolate compound coatings, molds do not like high heat. The dish washer will melt and warp your molds.

There are many great mold companies here in the United States and internationally. After thirty years of working with every different brand of chocolate mold I can get my hands on, I have become something of a mold snob. The molded confections in this book all use high performance chocolate making molds. Not high expensive chocolate making molds, just the right molds to be certain of your molding success. Collecting chocolate making molds is a hobby of mine.

Dipping Forks: As the name suggests, these forks will greatly assist you with most of your dipping needs. Dipping forks come in a variety of shapes. Rectangle, round, and ovals. They are made of plastic or metal. You may purchase them at candy specialty stores or our website.

Sheet Pans: Are commonly used in bakeries. The home version is a cookie sheet. Aluminum is best when working with confection. Keep them clean and clear of any debris.

Wax Paper and Parchment Paper: I prefer parchment paper. It holds up better than wax paper and can be used multiple times. I realize in some areas parchment paper is hard to come by and can be expensive, so wax paper is fine. Use wax or parchment paper every time you dip with the chocolate coatings and set them on a tray. This simple step will add a degree of professionalism to your creations as well as make clean up much easier. Be careful *not* to set your dipped confections on the edges of the paper. The chocolate coatings will swallow up the edges of the paper and it will be stuck inside your confection.

Wood Skewers: I recommend medium size wood skewers as a deposable paint brush. They work much better than tooth picks. Use then to apply the colored coatings and the details.

Paper Sticks and popsicle sticks create a lollypop. They make the favors convenient and easy to handle. They are available at craft stores and on line at our website.

Metal Clips are used to secure the molds when making three dimensional confections. You will find them at office supply stores.

Paring Knives: Small knives used for detail work. These knives are great for trimming finished confections.

From the kitchen:

Small spoons, stainless steel or plastic

Large spoons, stainless or plastic

Custard bowls, glass

Assorted sizes microwave safe bowls

Paper towels.

Spring Forward

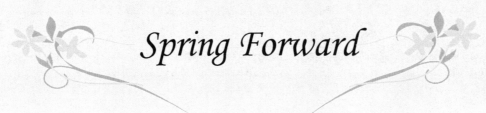

I can not resist all the wonderful flowers of spring. I look forward to this time of year knowing the weather is getting warmer and all of my favorite flowers will be blooming. With these chocolate flavored flowers and butterflies I can have spring any time of the year.

Daisy Favors	38
Butterfly Box	41
Butterfly Favors	43
Tulip Favors	44
Sunflower Favors	47
Rose Favors	48
Hibiscus Favors	50
Anthurium Favors	50
Ex Lg Sunflower	52
Calla Lilly Favors	55

1 Spring

Daisy Favors

Makes 21 daisy favors

One of the most popular flowers we offer. These daisy favors can be made with many different color combinations. Add a beautiful ribbon that accents your special event and give as party favors or make into bouquets.

3 cups pink coatings	1 daisy favor mold
1/2 cup milk coatings	21 four inch paper sticks
3 cups yellow coatings	21 two inch cello bags and ribbon (optional)
3 cups white coatings	

For daisy centers, place 1/2 cup of the pink coatings and the 1/2 cup milk coatings in separate microwave safe custard bowls. Microwave on 50% power for 30 second. Stir. Repeat until melted. Set bowls on a warm heating tray while you work. Using a medium skewer as a paint brush, apply the milk coatings to your brush and paint the center on all four of the favors in the mold applying more milk coatings as needed. Let dry.

Melt the remaining pink coatings as on page 20. When the centers are completely dry fill each favor cavity with pink coatings. Be careful not to overfill the favor cavity. Tap the mold gently on the counter. Place a four inch paper stick into each favor making sure the stick is at least one inch into the melted coatings. Refrigerate 15 to 20 minutes until favors release easily from mold. Repeat using different color combinations until you have the desired amount of favors. Let come to room temperature before you package with a cello bag and ribbon.

Butterfly Box

Makes 2 butterfly boxes

A wonderful gift all by its self or use these beautiful boxes as party favors or game prizes. Your friends and family will be so surprised they are edible boxes. Try hiding a small gift inside them.

1/2 cup pink coatings	2 ounces petite mints
1/2 cup yellow coatings	1 butterfly box mold
1/4 cup dark coatings	2 four inch cello bags and
3 cups milk coatings	ribbon (optional)
1 cup white coatings	

For the antenna and wings, place 1/2 cup of the pink coatings, 1/2 cup of the yellow coatings and the 1/4 cup dark coatings, in separate heat safe custard bowls. Microwave on 50% power for 30 second. Stir. Repeat until melted. Set bowls on a warm heating tray while you work. Using a medium skewer as a paint brush, apply dark coatings to your brush and paint the antenna and body of the butterfly. Applying more dark coatings when needed. Let dry. Using a small spoon, pour a small amount of pink coatings on the butterfly wings. Use a medium skewer to push the pink coatings into the wing details. Let dry.

Melt the milk and white coatings in separate bowls as on page 20. When the colors in the mold are completely dry, fill the bottom of the box with milk coatings, and then fill the top of the box with white coatings. Be careful not to overfill the cavities. Tap the mold gently on the counter. Refrigerate 30 to 40 minutes until top and bottom release easily from the mold. Repeat with yellow coatings. Fill with petite mints or other candy's. Let come to room temperature before you package with a cello bag and ribbon.

Note: The bottom of this mold needs to be cold before it will release from the mold. The top of this box may be poured with milk coatings.

Butterfly Favors

Makes 12 butterfly favors

So beautiful and fun at the same time. I try to keep these butterflies in the shop all year long. They have the mysterious ability of cheering us up each time we see them. Try replicating butterflies you have seen out doors. Some have spots, some have strips, all wonderful.

1/2 cup dark coatings

1 cup each, orange, yellow,

light green, and pink coatings

4 cups white coatings

1 butterfly mold

12 four inch paper sticks

12 three inch cello bags and ribbon (optional)

For the body, antennas and wings, place the dark coatings and assorted color coatings in separate, small microwave safe bowls. Microwave on 50% power for 30 second. Stir. Repeat until the coatings are melted. Set bowls on a warm heating tray while you work. Using a medium skewer as a paint brush, apply dark coatings to your brush and paint the body and antennas on all four of the favors in the mold, applying more coatings when needed. Let dry. With a small spoon, apply one of the colored coatings to all the wings on all four of the favors in the mold, applying more coatings when needed. Let dry.

Melt the white coatings as on page 20. When the colors in the mold are completely dry fill each favor cavity with white coatings. Be careful not to overfill favor cavities. Tap the mold gently on the counter. Place a four inch paper stick into each favor making sure the stick is at least one inch into the coatings. Refrigerate 15 to 20 minutes until favors release easily from mold. Repeat using different colors of coatings until you have the desired amount of favors. Let come to room temperature before you package with a cello bag and ribbon.

Tulip Favors

Makes 30 tulip favors

This is one of the simplest creations in this book, so I hope you will make them many times. In the photo we show beautiful pastels, but tulips come in so many different colors. Red, orange and milk chocolate tulips are beautiful as well. I like to use a soft green ribbon to represent the leaves or use your special event ribbon colors to pull the party together.

3 cups pink coatings	1 tulip favor mold
3 cups white coatings	30 four inch paper sticks
3 cups yellow coatings	30 two inch cello bags and ribbon (optional)

Melt the pink coatings as on page 20. Fill each tulip favor with pink coatings. Be careful not to overfill the favor cavity. Tap the mold gently on the counter. Place a four inch paper stick into each favor making sure the stick is at least one inch into the pink coatings. Refrigerate 15 to 20 minutes until the favors release easily from mold. Repeat using different colors of coatings until you have the desired amount of favors. Let come to room temperature before you package with a cello bag and ribbon.

Sunflower Favors

Makes 8 sunflower favors

This sunflower measures 5 1/4" in diameter and makes quite an impression as a party favor or in a flower arrangement. Choose an assortment of royal icing bugs or stay with a single theme like ladybugs. Any style of royal icing shapes will work on these sunflowers. You could use them for birthdays as well as baby showers by simply changing the royal icing shape.

1 cup milk coatings	8 eight inch paper sticks
5 cups yellow coatings	8 five inch cello bags and
8 royal icing bugs	and ribbon (optional)
1 sunflower mold	

Place the milk coatings in a small microwave safe bowl. Microwave on 50% power for 30 second. Stir. Repeat until coatings are melted. Set bowl on a warm heating tray while you work. Using a medium skewer as a paint brush, apply milk coatings to your brush and paint the center on the sunflower, applying more milk coatings when needed. Let dry.

Melt the yellow coatings as on page 20. When the milk coatings in the mold are completely dry, fill each sunflower cavity with yellow coatings. Be careful not to overfill favor cavity. Tap the mold gently on the counter. Place a eight inch stick into each favor making sure the stick is at least two inches into the coatings. Refrigerate 15 to 25 minutes until the sunflowers release easily from mold. Put a small drop of milk coatings on the back of the bug and place on the sunflower where ever you like. Press down lightly. Let dry. Let come to room temperature before you package with a cello bag and ribbon.

Open Rose Favors

Makes 15 favors

This simple yet elegant rose was discovered by my head chocolatier, Teresa. She has since retired but I could not retire this versatile party favor. Dress it up with beautiful ribbons and use for weddings, showers or Mother's Day.

2 cups pink coatings

2 cups white coatings

2 cups yellow coatings

1 open roses mold

15 six inch paper sticks

15 three inch cello bags

and ribbon (optional)

Melt the pink coatings as on page 20. Fill each favor cavity with pink coatings. Be careful not to overfill the favor cavity. Tap the mold gently on the counter. Place a six inch paper stick into each rose making sure the stick is at least one inch into the coatings. Refrigerate 15 to 20 minutes until the roses release easily from mold. Repeat using different colors of coatings until you have the desired amount of favors. Let come to room temperature before you package with a cello bag and ribbon.

Hibiscus and Anthurium Favors

Makes 14 favors

When I see Hibiscus or Anthuriums I am reminded of tropical places. I have made them for anniversary parties and special events that have a tropical theme. These flowers stay beautiful and fresh much longer than bouquets from the florist.

1 cup yellow coatings	1 hibiscus mold or 1 anthurium mold
4 cups pink coatings	14 six inch paper sticks
4 cups red coatings	14 three inch cello bags and ribbon (optional)

For Stamens, place 1 cup of the yellow coatings in a small microwave safe custard bowl. Microwave on 50% power for 30 second. Stir. Repeat until melted. Set bowl on a warm heating tray while you work. Using a medium skewer as a paint brush, apply the yellow coatings to your brush and paint the stamens on all of the favors in the mold, applying more yellow coatings when needed. Let dry.

Hibiscus Favor: Melt the pink coatings as on page 20. When the stamens are completely dry, fill each hibiscus cavity with pink coatings. Be careful not to overfill the favor cavity. Tap the mold gently on the counter. Place a six inch paper stick into each favor making sure the stick is at least two inches into the coatings. Refrigerate 15 to 20 minutes until favors release easily from mold. Let come to room temperature before you package with a cello bag and ribbon.

Anthurium Favor: Melt the red coatings as on page 20. When the stamens are completely dry fill each anthurium cavity with red coatings. Be careful not to overfill the favor cavity. Tap the mold gently on the counter. Place a six inch paper stick into each favor making sure the stick is at least two inches into the coatings. Refrigerate 15 to 20 minutes until favors release easily from mold. Let come to room temperature before you package with a cello bag and ribbon.

Extra Large Sunflowers

Makes 6 sunflower favors

These sunflowers will get everyone's attention. They measure 6½ inches in diameter. They are huge! Be sure to use a big ribbon on these.

1 cup milk coatings

7 cups yellow coatings

6 assorted royal icing bugs

1 large sunflower mold

6 twelve inch paper sticks

6 six inch cello bags and ribbon (optional)

For sunflower centers, place 1 cup of the milk coatings in a small microwave safe bowl. Microwave on 50% power for 30 second. Stir. Repeat until melted. Set bowl on a warm heating tray to hold while you work. Using a tea spoon apply milk coatings to the center of the sunflower. Applying more coatings as needed. Let dry completely. Melt the yellow coatings as on page 20. When the milk coatings are completely dry, fill each sunflower cavity with yellow coatings. Be careful not to overfill the favor cavity. Tap the mold gently on the counter. Place a twelve inch paper stick into the sunflower making sure the stick is at least four inches into the coatings. Refrigerate 15 to 30 minutes until sunflowers release easily from mold. Put a small drop of milk or yellow coatings on the back of the bug and place on the sunflower where ever you like. Press down lightly. Let dry. Let come to room temperature before you package with a cello bag and ribbon.

Large Calla Lily Favors

Makes 8 lily favors

Of all the flowers I can make in confection the lilies are the most elegant. This is a wonderful mold with correct detailing that gives this favor a three dimensional appearance. They are beautiful for Easter also.

1 cup yellow coatings

4 cups white coatings

1 calla lily mold

8 twelve inch paper sticks

8 - 2 x 7 inch cello bags and ribbon (optional)

For calla lily stamens, place 1 cup of the yellow coatings in a small microwave safe custard bowl. Microwave on 50% power for 30 second. Stir. Repeat until melted. Set bowl on a warm heating tray to hold while you work. Using a medium skewer as a paint brush, apply the yellow coatings to your brush and paint the stamens on all of the lilies in the mold, applying more coatings when needed. Let dry.

Melt the white coatings as on page 20. When the stamens are completely dry fill each calla lily cavity with white coatings. Be careful not to overfill the favor cavity. Tap the mold gently on the counter. Place a twelve inch paper stick into each favor making sure the stick is at least two inches into the coatings. Refrigerate 15 to 20 minutes until favors release easily from mold. Let come to room temperature before you package with a cello bag and ribbon.

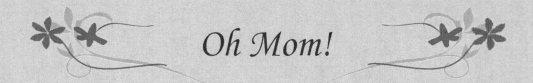

Oh Mom!

Of course many of the confections in this book would make great gifts and party favors for Mother's Day. But in this chapter I wanted to highlight a few extra special gifts. Only the best for Mother.

2

Mother's Day

Teacup and Teapot Favors

Makes 12 favors

We make these adorable Teacup and Teapot favors all year long. Ideal for the little girl's tea party as well as the grown-up tea party.

1/2 cup pink coatings	1 teacup/teapot mold
1/2 cup light green coatings	12 four inch paper sticks
5 cups white coatings	12 three inch cello bags and ribbon (optional)

For teapot and teacup roses, place 1/2 cup of the pink coatings and the 1/2 cup light green coatings in microwave safe custard bowls. Microwave on 50% power for 30 second. Stir. Repeat until melted. Set bowls on a warm heating tray while you work. Using a medium skewer as a paint brush, apply the pink coatings to your brush and paint the rose on all four of the favors in the mold, applying more pink coatings when needed. Let dry. Using the same technique, use a different brush and apply the light green coatings to all the leaves on all four of the favors in the mold, applying more light green coatings when needed. Let dry.

Melt the white coatings as on page 20. When the colors in the mold are completely dry fill each favor cavity with white coatings. Be careful not to overfill the favor cavity. Tap the mold gently on the counter. Place a four inch paper stick into each favor making sure the stick is at least one inch into the coatings. Refrigerate 15 to 20 minutes until favors release easily from mold. Let come to room temperature before you package with a cello bag and ribbon.

Teacup and Saucer

Makes 1 teacup and saucer

Looks like the real thing. This Teacup and Saucer are the same size as your china cups and saucers. One important difference is they taste much better. Fill with a favorite dessert or as shown here with assorted confections.

3 cups white coatings	4 dipped sandwich cookies, page 155
1 teacup mold	1 five inch cello bag and
1 saucer mold	ribbon (optional)
8 medal clips	

Melt the white coatings as on page 20. Using a tea spoon, fill the handle of both parts of the teacup mold with white coatings. Quickly put the right and left sides of the teacup together aliening all of the edges. Holding on its side, handle down, use the metal clips to secure the mold. Keeping the teacup handle side down and being careful to not let the white coatings drip out. Refrigerate for 15 minutes.

Fill the teacup half full with white coatings. Hold the teacup in your hand and roll your hand so the coatings cover the inside of the teacup. Use a teaspoon to push the coatings into open areas. Set in refrigerator for 10 minutes. Meanwhile, fill the saucer with white coatings being careful not to overfill. Refrigerate 20 minutes or until the saucer can be unmolded easily.

Remove the teacup mold from the refrigerator and add four heaping tablespoons of melted white coatings. Roll the coatings around the inside of the teacup again to make the walls of the teacup double thick. Set right side up in the refrigerator for 30 to 40 minutes until the teacup feels cold. To unmold the teacup, remove the clips. Insert your finger between the molds and slowly lift off the right and left sides.

Attach the teacup to the saucer by placing a small amount of white coatings on the center of the saucer and set the teacup on the melted white coatings and hold in place for one minute. Let dry completely. Fill with candy and decorate or fill with your favorite dessert and serve.

I like to put dipped cookies (page 155), mellows (page 152), a pink rose and a mini butterfly inside the Teacup for a special gift.

Sonia's Tips: The Teacup looks so real people will want to pick it up by the handle. Remember this is chocolate flavored coatings and the handle will break easily.

Mini Pink Roses

Makes 20 roses

Little roses to accompany your white Teacup or the top of cupcakes. There are so many uses for this confection. Set them on a dessert plate for added decoration.

2 cups pink coatings   1 mini rose mold

Melt the pink coatings as on page 20. Fill each rose cavity with pink coatings. Be careful not to overfill the rose cavity. Tap the mold gently on the counter. Refrigerate 15 to 20 minutes until the roses release easily from mold. Repeat with pink coatings until you have the desired number of roses. If desired, place in the Teacup on previous page. Store in an air tight container.

Mini Butterflies

Makes 24 butterflies

I wanted to share this mold with you because it adds the perfect accent to anything spring. Serve alone on a crystal dish or combine them with dipped cookies and mellows. Perhaps placed on cakes and cupcakes. I put them in the Teacup and Saucer found on page 60.

1 cup dark coatings

2 cups white coatings

2 cups pink coatings

2 cups yellow coatings

2 cups light green coatings

1 mini butterfly mold

For butterfly body's: Place 1 cup of the dark coatings in a small microwave safe bowl. Microwave on 50% power for 30 second. Stir. Repeat until melted. Set bowl on a warm heating tray while you work. Using a medium skewer as a paint brush, apply dark coatings to your brush and paint the body on all the butterflies in the mold, applying more dark coatings when needed. Let dry.

Melt the white coatings as on page 20. When the bodies are completely dry fill each butterfly cavity with white coatings. Be careful not to overfill the cavity. Tap the mold gently on the counter. Refrigerate 15 to 20 minutes until butterflies release easily from mold. Repeat using different colors of coatings until you have the desired number of butterflies. Store in an air tight container.

White Confection Swan

Makes 1 swan

A wonderful addition to your table or a terrific gift. This confection swan may be filled with assorted chocolates or your favorite dessert. I show it here as an edible fruit bowl. I recommend you read though the recipe before you start. These swans can be a little challenging.

5 cups white coatings

1 large swan mold

15 medal clips

1 eight inch cello bag and

ribbon (optional)

Melt the white coatings as on page 20. Using a large spoon fill the head and neck of both parts of the swan mold. Quickly put the right and left sides of the swan together aligning all of the edges. Turn the swan head side down being careful not to let the coatings drip out. Use the metal clips to secure the mold. Refrigerate for 15 minutes.

Fill the swan half full with white coatings. Holding the swan in your hands and roll the mold so the coatings cover the inside of the swan. Use a tea spoon to push the coatings into open areas. Set in refrigerator for 10 minutes. Add any remaining melted white coatings. Roll the coatings around the inside of the swan again to make the walls of the swan double thick. Set right side up in the refrigerator for 30 to 40 minutes until the swan feels cold. To unmold the swan, remove the clips, insert your finger between the molds and slowly lift off the right and left sides. Fill with your favorite fillings. Decorate with a cello bag and ribbon.

Rose Box

Makes 2 boxes

There are so many fun things you can do with these boxes. Hide a special gift of jewelry inside. Fill with your favorite dessert. Fill with chocolate mints and wrap with a cello bag and a beautiful ribbon. They are so beautiful most people do not realize they are edible.

1/2 cup pink coatings	4 ounces petite mints
1/4 cup light green coatings	1 rose box mold
3 cups milk coatings	2 four inch cello bags and
1 1/2 cups white coatings	ribbon (optional)

For the rose, place 1/2 cup of the pink coatings and the 1/4 cup light green coatings in separate microwave safe custard bowls. Microwave on 50% power for 30 second. Stir. Repeat until melted. Set bowls on a warm heating tray while you work. Using a medium skewer as a paint brush, apply the pink coatings to your brush and paint the rose in the mold, applying more coatings when needed. Let dry. Using the same technique, use a different brush and apply the light green to the leafs on the mold applying more coatings when needed. Let dry.

Melt the milk and white coatings in separate bowls as on page 20. When the colors in the mold are completely dry fill the bottom of the box with milk coatings and then fill the top of the box with white coatings. Be careful not to overfill the cavities. Tap the mold gently on the counter. Refrigerate 30 to 40 minutes until top and bottom release easily from the mold. The bottom of this mold needs to be cold before it will release from the mold. Fill with petite mints or other candies. Let come to room temperature before you package with a cello bag and ribbon. Note, the top of this box may be poured with milk coatings.

Happy Easter

I love everything about Easter and the confections for this holiday are too cute. I use these adorable confections to dress up my Easter table. Perfect for Easter baskets and gift giving at school or work. So many opportunities to share Easter joy.

Easter

Mellow Bunnies

Makes 10 bunnies

These bunnies are so cute I wish I could squeeze them. I like to put them in Easter baskets as an extra special treat. They work well in a cello bag with a ribbon too.

3 1/2 cups white coatings	1 mellow bunny mold
1 cup milk coatings	5 marshmallow cut in half
1/2 cup pink coatings	10 three inch cello bags and
1/4 cup dark coatings	ribbon (optional)

Mix together 1 1/2 cups of the white coatings with 1 cup of milk coating. Melt in a large bowl as on page 20. Stir until you have tan color. Set on a heating tray while you work. Fill the bunny's feet and head with tan coatings. Be careful not to overfill the cavities. Tap the mold gently on the counter. Refrigerate 15 to 20 minutes until bunnies release easily from mold. Set the bunny heads and feet on a cookie sheet. Repeat with white coatings.

Place the pink and dark coatings in separate small microwave safe bowls. Microwave on 50% power for 30 seconds. Stir. Repeat until coatings are melted. Set on a heating tray while you work. Using a medium skewer as a paint brush, apply pink coatings to your brush and paint the nose and ears on all of the bunny faces, applying more coatings when needed. Let dry. Using the same technique, paint the bunny eyes with the dark coatings on all of the bunny faces, applying more coatings when needed. Let dry.

For the body, dip 5 marshmallow halves into the melted white coatings. Set on wax paper and cool for 10 minutes in the refrigerator. Repeat with tan the coatings.

Assembling the bunnies: Set all parts of the bunny together on a cookie sheet. Place a dime size amount of like colored coatings onto one of the bunnies feet. Set a like colored marshmallow half onto the feet portion of the bunny. Repeat for all bunnies.

Place a dime size amount of like colored coatings onto the back side of a bunny head. Place the head onto a like colored marshmallow and hold for a few seconds until it stays.

Let come to room temperature before you package with a cello bag and ribbon.

Confection Carrots

Makes 12 assorted carrots

These confection carrots are very versatile. Use them for edible decorations or pass them out as bunny food. The small carrots in this recipe are used to fill the wheel barrow on page 89.

1 cup green coatings

4 cups orange coatings

1 carrot mold

12 two inch cello bags and ribbon (optional)

Place the green coatings in a small microwave safe bowl. Microwave on 50% power for 30 seconds. Stir. Repeat until coatings are melted. Set on a warm heating tray while you work. Using a Medium skewer as a paint brush, apply green coatings to your brush and paint the leaf area on all of the carrots in the mold, applying more coatings when needed. Let dry.

Melt the orange coatings in a large bowl as on page 20. When the colors in the mold are completely dry, fill the carrots with orange coatings. Be careful not to overfill cavities. Tap the mold gently on the counter. Refrigerate 15 to 20 minutes until the carrots release easily from mold. Repeat until you have the desired amount of carrots. Let come to room temperature before you package with a cello bag and ribbon.

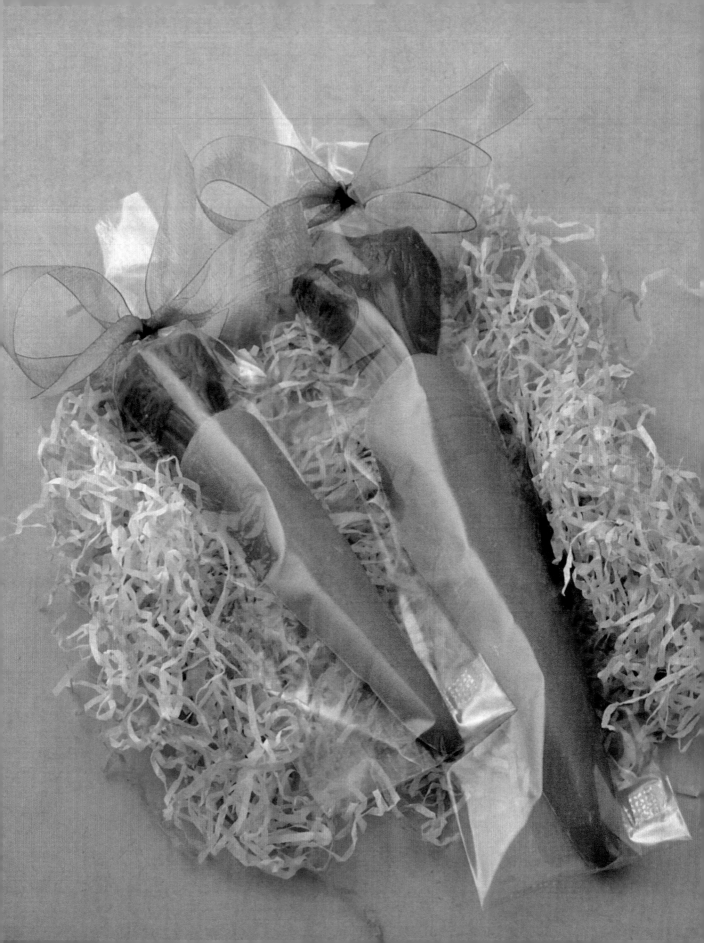

Girl Bunny Favor

Makes 12 bunnies

I've been making this sweet girl bunny for many years. This girl bunny and the boy bunny on the following page are part of my private collection. I am very happy to be able to share them with you.

1 cup pink coatings	1 girl bunny mold
1/2 cup yellow coatings	12 four inch paper sticks
1/2 cup dark coatings	12 two inch tall cello bags and
5 cups white coatings	ribbon (optional)

Place pink, yellow and dark coatings in separate small microwave safe bowls. Microwave on 50% power for 30 seconds. Stir. Repeat until coatings are melted. Set on a heating tray while you work. Using a medium skewer as a paint brush, apply pink coatings to your brush and paint the nose, two of the flowers and the ribbon on all of the bunnies in the mold, applying more coatings when needed. Let dry. Using the same technique, use a different brush and apply the yellow coatings to the remaining two flowers on bunnies in the mold, applying more coatings when needed. Let dry.

Melt the white coatings as on page 20. When the colors in the mold are completely dry fill the bunnies with white coatings. Be careful not to overfill cavities. Insert a four inch paper stick. Tap the mold gently on the counter. Refrigerate 15 to 20 minutes until bunnies release easily from mold. Dot the center of the flowers with contrasting coatings. Repeat until you have the desired amount of bunnies.

For the eyes: Use a medium skewer and apply the dark coatings to all the eyes on the bunnies, applying more coatings when needed.

Let come to room temperature before you package with a cello bag and ribbon.

Boy Bunny Favor

Makes 12 Boy Bunnies

This Boy Bunny is the partner to the Girl Bunny on the previous page. Ready to go with his basket full of flowers. Check out page 74 for the small carrots shown in the photo.

1/4 cup blue coatings	5 cups white coatings
1/4 cup pink coatings	1 boy bunny mold
1/4 cup yellow coatings	12 four inch paper sticks
1/4 cup dark coatings	12 four inch tall cello bags and
1/4 cup green coatings	ribbon (optional)
1/4 cup milk coatings	

Place the blue, pink, yellow, dark, green and milk coatings in separate microwave safe custard bowls. Microwave on 50% power for 30 seconds. Stir. Repeat until coatings are melted. Set on a heating tray while you work. Using a medium skewer as a paint brush, apply blue coatings to your brush and paint the ribbon and one flower. Using the same technique, use a different brush and apply the pink coatings to all the noses and one flower, applying more coatings when needed. Using the same technique again, use a different brush and apply the yellow coatings to the remaining flower on bunnies in the mold, applying more coatings when needed. Let dry. When the flowers are dry use your brush and paint the green coatings onto the leaves. Let dry.

Melt the white coatings as on page 20. Add a few teaspoons of white coatings to the melted milk coatings and stir. You are creating tan for the basket. When the flowers are completely dry, apply the tan coatings to the basket portion in the mold, applying more coatings when needed. Let dry.

When the colors in the mold are completely dry, fill the bunnies with white coatings. Be careful not to overfill cavities. Insert four inch paper stick. Tap the mold gently on the counter. Refrigerate 15 to 20 minutes until bunnies release easily from mold. Repeat until you have the desired amount of bunnies.

For the eyes and ears: use a medium skewer and apply the dark coatings to all the eyes on the bunnies, applying more coatings when needed. Using the same technique paint the ears with the pink coatings. Let dry.

Let come to room temperature before you package with a cello bag and ribbon.

Easter Basket with Handle

Makes 1 basket

I fill this basket with dipped mellows and dipped sandwich cookies. Both recipes are in chapter 6 on dipping. The carrots on page 74 look great in the basket too.

2 1/2 cups white coatings	assorted confections to fill
2 1/2 cups milk coatings	the basket
1 basket with handle mold	1 seven inch cello bags and
16 metal clips	ribbon (optional)

Combined the milk and the white coatings in a large microwave safe bowls and melt as on page 20. Stir well until you have a tan color. Beginning with the basket handle, spoon coatings into both handle sides. Filling the handles as much as possible. In this case, it is ok if a little of the coatings overflow. Holding one side of the mold in your left hand, pick up the other side with your right hand and quickly put the top half onto the bottom half. Align all of the edges. Holding on its side so the handle stays full of coatings, apply the metal clips to all sides of the basket. Tab gently on the side of the counter to pack the coatings and release air bubbles. Take time now to fill the handles with as much tan coatings as they will hold. Holding the basket upside down spoon the coatings into the base of the handle. Set in the refrigerator, upside down, for 20 minutes or until the handle is cool and set.

Remove the basket from the refrigerator being cartful not to squeeze or bend it. Holding right side up, pour enough coatings into it so it is half full. Roll the mold around gently so the coatings cover the entire insides, the rim, and touches the coatings in the handle. Check for air bubbles in the basket by holding it at eye level and inspecting all sides. Use a spoon to push the air bubbles out of the basket. Set in the refrigerator for 15 minutes. Add more coatings and roll the coatings around the mold so that it covers all of the inside. Refrigerate for 10 minutes. Roll the coatings around the inside of the mold and refrigerate 40 minutes or until it is cold.

When the mold feels cold to the touch take it out of the refrigerator and remove the clips. Gently insert your fingers between the molds and try lifting off the top. This should be very simple. If they do not easily come apart, return the basket to the refrigerator for 15 minutes and try to remove the molds again. Note: If your basket will not stand up on its own, use a paring knife to level the bottom of the basket.

Let come to room temperature. Fill with your favorite candy and package with a cello bag and ribbon.

Sonia's Tips; Remember not to hold the basket by the handle. It may break.

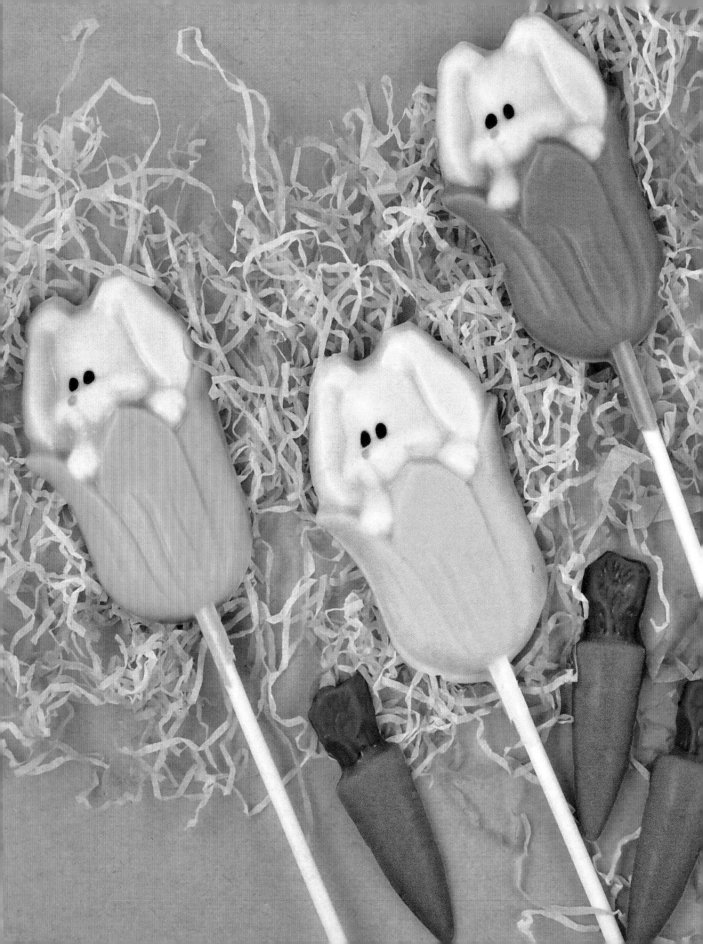

Tulip Bunny

Makes 12 bunnies

Sweet to look at, sweet to eat. Slightly smaller than the other Easter favors but they make up for it in cuteness.

1 cup pink coatings

1 cup yellow coatings

1 cup light green coatings

3 cups white coatings

1/4 cup dark coatings

1 tulip bunny mold

12 four inch paper sticks

12 two inch cello bags and

ribbon (optional)

Place pink, yellow, light green and dark coatings in separate small microwave safe bowls. Microwave on 50% power for 30 seconds. Stir. Repeat until the coatings are melted. Set on a heating tray while you work. Using a medium skewer as a paint brush, apply pink coatings to your brush and paint the nose, and the tulip potion of the mold, applying more coatings when needed. Let dry.

Melt the white coatings as on page 20. When the colors in the mold are completely dry, fill the bunnies with white coatings. Be careful not to overfill cavities. Insert four inch paper stick. Tap the mold gently on the counter. Refrigerate 15 to 20 minutes until bunnies release easily from mold. Repeat with different colors until you have the desired amount of bunnies.

For the eyes: Use a medium skewer and apply the dark coatings to all the eyes on the bunnies, applying more coatings when needed.

Let come to room temperature before you package with a cello bag and ribbon.

Large Brown Bunny

Makes 2 bunnies

I have made these brown bunnies to put in gift basket and some of my customers ship them over sea's to their family in the military. They weigh 10 ounces. Any chocolate lover would be happy to receive one of these.

1/2 cup pink coatings	2 small orange carrots from page 74
1/4 cup white coatings	1 brown bunny mold
1/4 cup dark coatings	2 five inch cello bags and
3 cups milk coatings	ribbon (optional)

Place pink, white and dark coatings in separate small microwave safe bowls. Microwave on 50% power for 30 seconds. Stir. Repeat until the coatings are melted. Set on a heating tray while you work. Using a medium skewer as a paint brush, apply pink coatings to your brush and paint the nose and the pawn potions of the mold, applying more coatings when needed. Let dry. Using the same technique paint the eye area with white coatings. Let dry.

Melt the milk coatings as on page 20. When the colors in the mold are completely dry, fill the bunnies with milk coatings. Be careful not to overfill the cavity. Tap the mold gently on the counter. Refrigerate 20 to 25 minutes until bunny releases easily from mold. Repeat to make one more bunny.

For the eyes: use a medium skewer and apply the dark coatings to resemble the retina of the eye.

Using the coatings as 'glue' place a small amount of milk coatings where the bunnies hands are. Set the carrot on the hands and let dry. Let come to room temperature before you package with a cello bag and ribbon.

Confection Wheel Barrow

Makes 4 wheel barrows

In this recipe you will be using white coatings for glue. When you are finished building this wheel barrow you will want to put it in a highly visible place. It is just that cute. It also make a great dessert bowl.

1 cup pink coatings	20 small orange carrots from page 74
1/4 cup yellow coatings	1 wheel barrow mold
1/4 cup light green coatings	4 four inch cello bags and
4 cups white coatings	ribbon (optional)

Place pink, yellow and light green coatings in separate small microwave safe bowls. Microwave on 50% power for 30 seconds. Stir. Repeat until coatings are melted. Set on a heating tray while you work. Using a medium skewer as a paint brush, apply yellow coatings to your brush and paint the center of the flowers, applying more coatings when needed. Let dry. Fill the flowers with pink coatings. Be careful not to overfill cavities.

Melt the white coatings as on page 20. Carefully fill the wheel barrel pieces in the mold. They are shallow and will not require a lot of coatings. Less is better here. Tap the mold gently on the counter. Refrigerate 15 to 20 minutes until wheel barrow pieces release easily from mold. Repeat until you have the desired amount of wheel barrows. Use assorted colors for the flowers to your preference.

Wheel barrow assembly: Place all the wheel barrow parts on a cookie sheet. Place a quarter size amount of white coatings in the middle of the base. Set the box on top of it. On each flower place a drop of white coatings and 'glue' them to both sides of the wheel barrow box as in the photograph. Place a small drop of white coatings on the back side of a wheel piece. Press the two sides of the wheel together keeping the lines on both side even. Put a drop of coatings on the inside area of the wheel well. Pick up the front of the wheel barrow and push the wheel into that area holding up to 5 seconds or until it stays in position. Add the five small carrots. Package with a cello bag and ribbon.

Sonia's Tips: Since the wheel barrel is completely edible it can also be used as part of your dessert. Fill it with something cold like pistachio pudding.

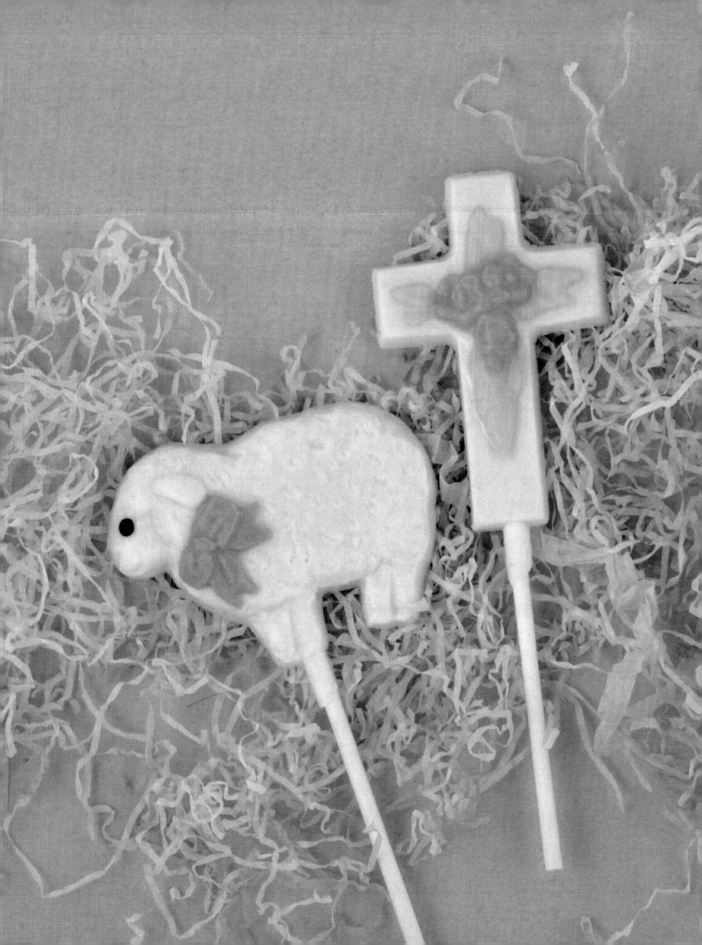

Easter Lamb Favor

Makes 12 lambs

Little lambs are perfect for Easter. These lambs are a little less effort than some of the other Easter favors. Very kid friendly.

1/2 cup pink coatings	4 cups white coatings
1/2 cup yellow coatings	1 Easter Lamb mold
1/2 cup light green coatings	12 four inch paper sticks
1/2 cup blue coatings	12 three inch cello bags and
1/4 cup dark coatings	ribbon (optional)

Place pink, yellow, light green, blue and dark coatings in separate microwave safe custard bowls. Microwave on 50% power for 30 seconds. Stir. Repeat until the coatings are melted. Set on a heating tray while you work. Using a medium skewer as a paint brush, apply pink coatings to your brush and paint the nose and the ribbon on all four of the lambs in the mold, applying more coatings when needed. Let dry. Using the same technique and a fresh skewer, paint the eyes with dark coatings.

Melt the white coatings as on page 20.   When the colors in the mold are completely dry fill the lambs with white coatings. Be careful not to overfill cavities. Insert a four inch paper stick. Tap the mold gently on the counter. Refrigerate 15 to 20 minutes until lambs release easily from mold. Repeat with different colors until you have the desired amount of lambs. Let come to room temperature before you package with a cello bag and ribbon.

For the tan lambs, melt together 2 cups white coating and 1 cup milk coatings. Replace for the white coatings.

Cross Favor

We make hundreds of these cross favors at Easter. I hope you enjoy them as much as we have.

1/2 cup pink coatings	1 cross favor mold
1/2 cup light green coatings	12 four inch paper sticks
1/2 cup blue coatings	12 three inch cello bags and
2 cups white coatings	ribbon (optional)
2 cups milk coatings	

Place pink, light green and blue coatings in separate microwave safe custard bowls. Microwave on 50% power for 30 seconds. Stir. Repeat until the coatings are melted. Set on a heating tray while you work. Using a medium skewer as a paint brush, apply pink coatings to your brush and paint the roses in all four crosses in the mold, applying more coatings when needed. Let dry. Using the same technique and a fresh skewer, paint the leaves with light green coatings.

Melt the white and milk coatings in separate bowls as on page 20. When the colors in the mold are completely dry fill the crosses with white coatings. Be careful not to overfill the cavities. Insert a four inch paper stick. Tap the mold gently on the counter. Refrigerate 15 to 20 minutes until crosses release easily from mold. Repeat with different colors until you have the desired amount of crosses.

Let come to room temperature before you package with a cello bag and ribbon.

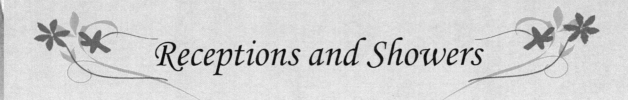

Receptions and Showers

Adding a ribbon with your event colors to any of the beautiful confections in this chapter will help create a wonderful party atmosphere.

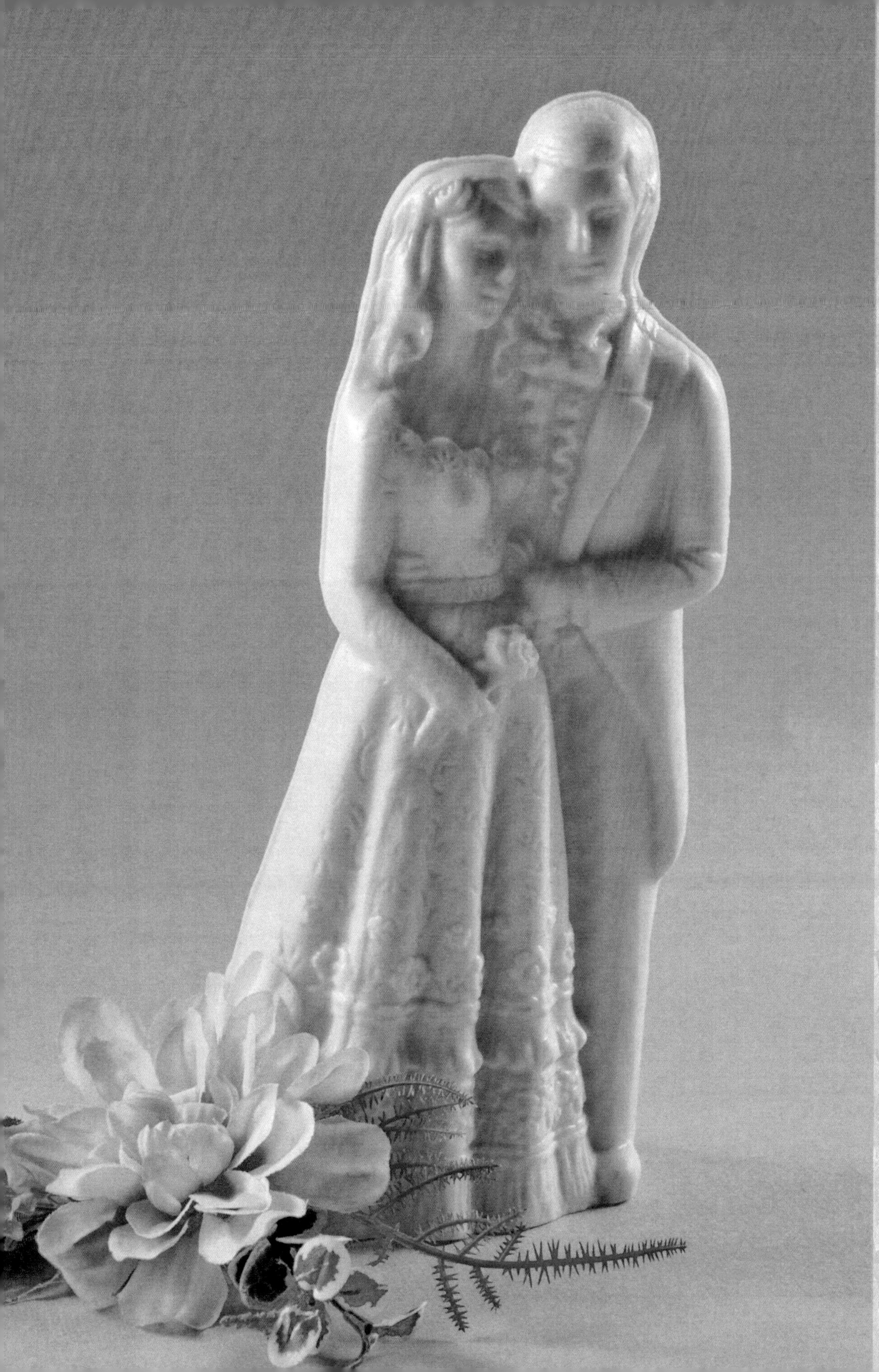

4 Wedding & Baby

Bride and Groom Statue

Makes 1 statue

This statue will get lots of attention. Many of my brides like to set it on the cake table. I hope you will take a minute to notice the detailing. It is a work of art.

5 cups white coatings

1 bride and groom statue mold

1- 5 x 15 inch cello bag and

ribbon (optional)

Melt the white coatings as on page 20. Beginning with the back half of the mold, pour 2 cups of white coatings into the mold half. With a spoon push the white coatings around the mold to cover it completely with coatings. Tap the mold on the counter. Hold the mold up so you can see under the mold and no coatings pours out. Check for air bubbles. Use the spoon to push any air bubbles out. Next, pour enough coatings into the back half of the mold so it is 3/4 full. Set aside where it will not tip over. Use the remaining white coatings in the front half. Repeat the process with the front half of the mold. Set aside where it will not tip over. Hold the back half of the statue in your left hand. Pick up the front half of the statue in your right. In a quick motion put the front half onto the bottom half. Be sure to align all the edges. Apply the metal clips to all sides of the bottle. Once you have the clips in place and are sure the coatings will not drip out, roll the mold around gently so the coatings cover the entire insides of the statue. Set on its side, in the refrigerator for 15 minutes.

Take the statue out of the refrigerator and rotate it so coatings move around the inside of the statue. Turn upside down for 5 seconds to let the coatings move to the top of the statue. Turn over and refrigerate 15 more minutes. Turn over once more and refrigerate 15 more minutes or until it has cooled enough to remove from mold.

When the mold feels cold to the touch, take it out of the refrigerator and remove the clips. Gently insert your fingers between the molds and try lifting off the top. This should be very simple. If they do not easily come apart return to the refrigerator for 15 minutes and try to remove the molds again. Note: if your statue will not stand up on its own, use a paring knife to level the bottom of the statue. Let come to room temperature before you package with a cello bag and ribbon.

Wedding Cake Favor

Makes 12 cakes

This is a favorite at Chocolates By imagination. It looks great with any color ribbon, even white. They are simple to make and dress up any reception table. This recipe will easily double, triple or more depending on how many you need. 300 for a wedding? Absolutely. There are four cake favors on a mold. If you will be making a large amount, I recommend getting three or four molds. I show a variety of styles here. You may choose to use one for your event or several styles.

4 cups white coatings	12 paper sticks (optional)
1 wedding cake mold or	12 three inch cello bags
your preferred mold choice	ribbon (optional)

Melt the white coatings as on page 20. Fill each cake cavity with white coatings. Be careful not to overfill the favor cavity. Tap the mold gently on the counter. Place a four inch paper stick into each cake making sure the stick is at least one inch into the coatings. Refrigerate 15 to 20 minutes until the cakes release easily from mold. Repeat until you have the desired number of favors. Let come to room temperature before you package with a cello bag and ribbon.

Sonia's Tips: The paper stick is optional. I recommend if you are going to pass out the favors or put them in a basket use the paper stick. If you will be placing them at each table setting they are quite beautiful without the paper stick.

Brides Dress and Grooms Tux Favors

Makes 24 favors

These favors are just too cute. Perfect for wedding showers and wedding receptions. I show several ways to make them, some with added color some poured plain. Ether way very elegant.

1/4 cup pink coatings	1 grooms tux mold
4 cups white coatings	24 six inch paper stick
4 cups dark coatings	24 two inch cello bags and
1 brides dress mold	ribbon

Wedding Dress: If you are going to put accent colors on the wedding dress, place the pink coatings in a microwave safe custard bowl. Microwave on 50% power for 30 seconds. Stir. Repeat until the coatings are melted. Set on a heating tray while you work. Using a medium skewer as a paint brush, apply pink coatings to your brush and paint the flowers on all the wedding dresses in the mold, applying more coatings when needed. Let dry. Continue with the next stage.

For pouring white wedding dresses with no accent colors start here.

Set aside 1/2 cup of white coatings. Melt the remaining white coatings as on page 20. Fill each favor cavity with white coatings. Be careful not to overfill the dress cavity. Tap the mold gently on the counter. Place a six inch paper stick into each favor making sure the stick is at least one inch into the coatings. Refrigerate 15 to 20 minutes until the favors release easily from mold. Let come to room temperature before you package with a cello bag and ribbon.

Grooms Tux: Place 1/2 cup white coatings and 1/2 cup dark coatings in separate microwave safe custard bowls. Microwave on 50% power for 30 seconds. Stir. Repeat until the coatings are melted. Set on a heating tray while you work. Using a medium skewer as a paint brush, apply dark coatings to your brush and paint the bow tie area on all the tux in the mold, applying more coatings when needed. Let dry. Using the same technique, use a different brush and apply the pink coatings to all the boutonnieres and the white coatings to the shirts on all the favors in the mold, applying more coatings when needed. Let dry.

Melt the remaining dark coatings as on page 20. Fill each favor cavity with dark coatings. Be careful not to overfill the cavity. Tap the mold gently on the counter. Place a six inch paper stick into each favor making sure the stick is at least one inch into the coatings. Refrigerate 15 to 20 minutes until the favors release easily from mold. Let come to room temperature before you package with a cello bag and ribbon.

Cherub Heart Box

Makes 2 boxes

This mold has been with me from the very beginning. It is a timeless piece that I make year around. Filled here with petite mints, but feel free to use your favorite sweets.

> 4 cups white coatings
>
> 1 cherub heart box mold
>
> 2 ounces petite mints
>
> 2 four inch cello bags and
>
> ribbon (optional)

Melt the white coatings as on page 20. Fill the bottom section of the mold first with white coatings. Be careful not to overfill the cavity. Tap mold gently on the counter. Fill the top section of the cherub box being careful not to overfill the cavity. Set in refrigerate on a level shelf for 20 to 30 minutes until cherub box releases easily from mold. Let come to room temperature before you package with a cello bag and ribbon.

Sonia's tips: The top of this cherub box will easily over flow. It is better to under fill the top. Also, when you add mint candy to the confection box, the white confection will absorb the mint flavor and aroma and taste like mint. If you wish to avoid this, choose a candy without a strong flavor such as candy coated chocolates.

Ducky Favor

Bright yellow baby ducks perfect for baby showers. Add a pink or blue ribbon if you want to reveal the gender of the baby. If not yellow and mint green look beautiful too.

1/4 cup orange coatings	1 ducky mold
1/4 cup dark coatings	12 four inch paper sticks
4 cups yellow coatings	12 three inch cello bags ribbon

Place orange and dark coatings in separate microwave safe custard bowls. Microwave on 50% power for 30 seconds. Stir. Repeat until the coatings are melted. Set on a heating tray while you work. Using a medium skewer as a paint brush, apply orange coatings to your brush and paint the beaks on all three of the favors in the mold, applying more coatings when needed. Let dry. Using the same technique, use a different brush and apply the dark coatings to the eyes on all three of the favors in the mold, applying more coatings when needed. Let dry.

Melt the yellow coatings as on page 20. When the colors in the mold are completely dry fill each favor cavity with yellow coatings. Be careful not to overfill ducky cavity. Tap the mold gently on the counter. Place a four inch paper stick into each favor making sure the stick is at least one inch into the coatings. Refrigerate 15 to 20 minutes until the favor release easily from mold. Let come to room temperature before you package with a cello bag and ribbon.

Baby Lamb Favor

Makes 12 lambs

I know this Baby Lamb wants to go home with you. Many of my customers have trouble deciding which baby favor to use for their baby showers. I say use as many different styles as you like. The Lamb and Ducky favors go well together.

1/4 cup pink coatings	1 baby lamb favor mold
1/4 cup dark coatings	12 four inch paper sticks
4 cups white coatings	12 three inch cello bags and ribbon (optional)

Place pink and dark coatings in separate microwave safe custard bowl. Microwave on 50% power for 30 seconds. Stir. Repeat until the coatings are melted. Set on a heating tray while you work. Using a medium skewer as a paint brush, apply pink coatings to your brush and paint the nose and ears on all four of the favors in the mold, applying more coatings when needed. Let dry. Using the same technique, use a different brush and apply the dark coatings to the eyes and the hoofs on all four of the favors in the mold, applying more coatings when needed. Let dry. Melt the white

coatings as on page 20. When the colors in the mold are completely dry fill each lamb cavity with white coatings. Be careful not to overfill the cavity. Tap the mold gently on the counter. Place a four inch paper stick into each favor making sure the stick is at least one inch into the coatings. Refrigerate 15 to 20 minutes until the lambs release easily from mold. Let come to room temperature before you package with a cello bag and ribbon.

Baby Bottle

Makes 2 bottles

I recommend to my customers and friends to use these Baby Bottles as game prizes. Wrap them in a cello bag with a beautiful ribbon for a perfect gift. Most people have never seen anything like them.

1/2 cup pink coatings

1/2 blue coatings

4 cups white coatings

1 tall baby bottle mold

16 metal clips

2 four inch cello bags and

ribbon (optional)

Place the pink and blue coatings in separate small microwave safe bowls. Microwave on 50% power for 30 seconds. Stir. Repeat until completely melted. Set on a heating tray while you work. Using a medium skewer as a paint brush, apply the pink coatings to your brush and paint the bottle cap section of the bottle . Being carefully to keep the edges smooth. Applying more coatings when needed. Let dry.

Melt the white coatings as on page 20. Beginning with the back half of the bottle mold, pour enough coatings into the mold so it is 3/4 full. Set aside where it will not tip over. Holding the front half of the bottle, pour enough coatings into it so it is 1/4 full. Set aside where it will not tip over. Hold the back half of the bottle mold in your left hand. Pick up the front half of the bottle in your right. In a quick motion put the front half on top of the back half. Be sure to align the edges. Apply the metal clips to all sides of the bottle. Once you have the clips in place and are sure the coatings will not drip out, roll the mold around gently so the coatings cover the entire insides of the bottle. Set on its side, in the refrigerator for 15 minutes.

Take the bottle out of the refrigerator and rotate so the coatings move around the inside of the bottle. Turn upside down for 5 seconds to let coatings move to the top of the bottle. Turn over and refrigerate 15 more minutes. Turn over once more and refrigerate 15 more minutes or until it has cooled enough to remove from mold.

When the mold feels cold to the touch, take it out of the refrigerator and remove the clips. Gently insert you finger between the molds and try lifting off the top. This should be very simple. If they do not come apart easily return to the refrigerator for 15 minutes and try to remove the molds again. Note: if your bottle will not stand up on its own, use a paring knife to level the bottom of the bottle. Let come to room temperature before you package with a cello bag and ribbon.

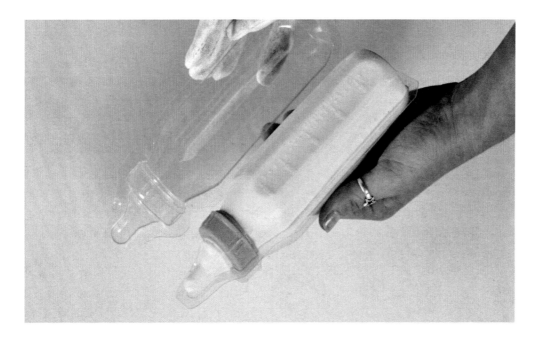

Sonia's Tips: The blue and the pink coatings in this recipe are just suggestions. Yellow, light green and lavender also look great.

Baby in Blanket Favor

Makes 16 babies

Just when I thought confection could not get any more adorable, these adorable babies come along. I like to make their hair different colors brown, black or blond to resemble Mom and Dad.

2 cups yellow coatings	2 cups light green coatings
1/4 cup milk coatings	1 baby in blanket mold
1/4 cup dark coatings	16 four inch paper sticks
1/2 cup white coatings	16 three inch cello bags and
2 cups pink coatings	ribbon (optional)
2 cups blue coatings	

Place yellow, milk and dark coatings in separate microwave safe small bowls. Microwave on 50% power for 30 seconds. Stir. Repeat until the coatings are melted. Set on a heating tray while you work. Using a medium skewer as a paint brush, apply dark coatings to your brush and paint the eyes on all four of the favors in the mold, applying more coatings when needed. Let dry. Using the same technique, paint the hair with yellow coatings. Let dry.

For the baby's skin; Place the white coatings in a small microwave safe bowl. Microwave on 50% power for 30 seconds. Stir. Repeat until the coatings are melted. Add small drops of the melted milk coatings to the white and stir continually until you have the 'skin' color of your preference. Keep in mind this color will be darker when it cools. Using a medium skewer as a paint brush, apply the skin color coatings to your brush and paint the face and feet of the baby's on all four of the favors in the mold, applying more coatings when needed. Let dry.

Melt the light green coatings as on page 20. When the color in the mold is completely dry fill each baby cavity with light green coatings. Be careful not to overfill the cavity. Tap the mold gently on the counter. Place a four inch paper stick into each favor making sure the stick is at least one inch into the coatings. Refrigerate 15 to 20 minutes until the favors releases easily from mold. Repeat with the different colors of coatings until you have the desired number of favors. Let come to room temperature before you package with a cello bag and ribbon.

Baby Bottle Favor

Makes 15 bottles

The baby bottle favor is the smallest of the favors in this chapter, but they put on a big show and are easily added to any baby event. Use a combination of white coatings and milk coatings for added interest.

1/2 cup pink coatings	1 baby bottle favor mold
1/2 cup blue coatings	15 four inch paper sticks
3 cups white coatings	15 two inch cello bags and
3 cups milk coatings	ribbon (optional)

Place pink and blue coatings in separate microwave safe custard bowls. Microwave on 50% power for 30 seconds. Stir. Repeat until the coatings are melted. Set on a heating tray while you work. Using a medium skewer as a paint brush, apply pink coatings to your brush and paint the cap on all five of the favors in the mold, applying more coatings when needed. Let dry.

Melt the white coatings as on page 20. When the color in the mold is completely dry fill each bottle cavity with white coatings. Be careful not to overfill the cavity. Tap the mold gently on the counter. Place a four inch paper stick into each favor making sure the stick is at least one inch into the coatings. Refrigerate 15 to 20 minutes until the favors release easily from mold. Repeat with blue and milk coatings until you have the desired number of favors. Let come to room temperature before you package with a cello bag and ribbon.

Baby Bootie

Makes 4 booties

This Bootie is the prefect size for party favors or party prizes. I filled them with candy baby rattles but assorted mints or whatever you like will be delicious as well.

1/2 cup pink coatings	4 ounces baby rattle candies
5 cups white coatings	4 four inch cello bags and
1 baby bootie mold	ribbon (optional)

Place the pink coatings in a microwave safe custard bowl. Microwave on 50% power for 30 seconds. Stir. Repeat until the coatings are melted. Set on a heating tray while you work. Using a medium skewer as a paint brush, apply pink coatings. Melt the white coatings as on page 20. When the color in the mold is completely dry fill each bootie cavity with white coatings. Be careful not to overfill the cavity. Tap the mold gently on the counter. Refrigerate 15 to 20 minutes until the favor releases easily from mold. Fill each bootie with one ounce of candy. Repeat until you have the desired number of favors. Let come to room temperature before you package with a cello bag and ribbon.

Bon Voyage

Confections are often overlooked when it comes to summer. And with all the parties and get togethers there is so much opportunity. Yes, you need to keep them cool so keep them in a cool place.

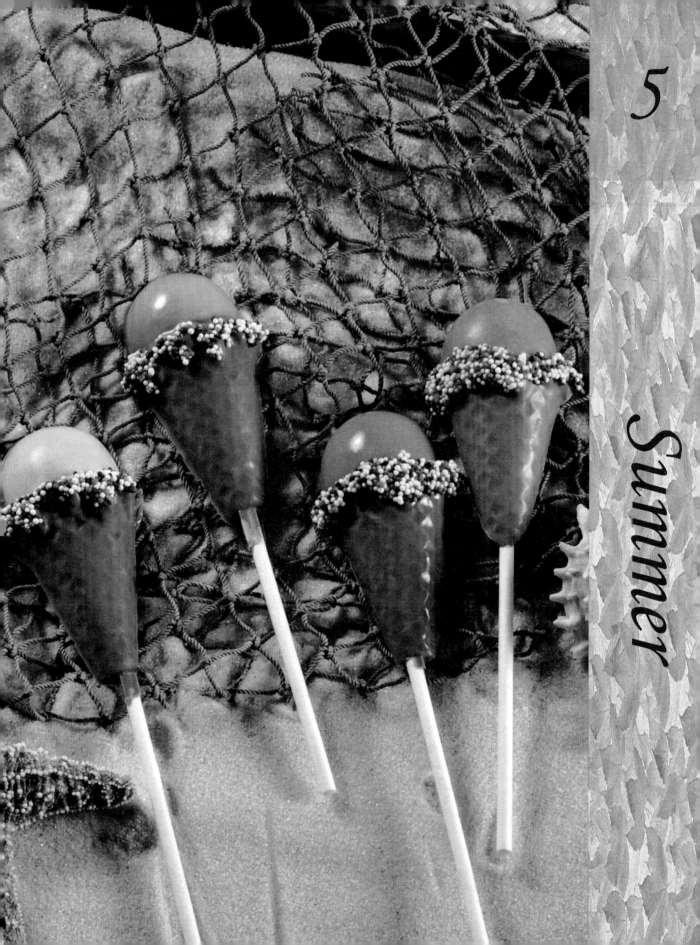

5

Summer

Ice Cream Cones

Makes 15 ice creams

A summer time favorite and super cute. I love the way the mold for this favor shows the cone pattern and that makes them look like the real thing. I have accented these cones with multi colored non pariels but feel free to use any topping you like.

1/2 cup pink coatings	1 1/2 cups milk coatings
1/2 cup yellow coatings	5 ounces multi colored non pariels
1/2 cup green coatings	1 ice cream cone mold
1/2 cup orange coatings	15 six inch paper sticks
3 cups white coatings	15 two inch cello bags and ribbon

Place the pink, yellow, green and orange coatings in separate small microwave safe bowls. Melt in microwave on 50% power for 30 seconds. Stir. Repeat until melted. Place on a warm heating tray while you are working. Using a medium skewer as a paint brush, apply the pink coatings to your brush and paint the ice cream part on all five of the ice creams in the mold, applying more coatings when needed. Let dry.

Place the white coatings and milk coatings together in a large microwave safe bowl. Melt in microwave as on page 20. Stir until both colors are completely mixed and you have a tan color. When the ice creams are completely dry, fill each ice cream cone with tan coatings. Be careful not to overfill favor cavity. Tap the mold gently on the counter. Place a six inch paper stick into each favor making sure the stick is at least one inch into the coatings. Refrigerate 15 to 20 minutes until favors release easily from mold. Repeat using different colors of coatings until you have the desired number of favors.

Arrange your cones on a cookie sheet. Pour the non pariels in to a shallow bowl. One favor at a time, using your skewer, apply a line of melted tan coatings along the top of the cone. Dip the cone into the non pariels so the non pariels stick to the tan coating. Set on a cookie sheet to let dry. Let come to room temperature before you package with a cello bag and ribbon.

Chocolate Fudge Bar

Makes 12 fudge bars

Fudge bars were my favorite ice cream as a kid. Adding the popsicle stick makes these chocolate flavored fudge bars look like the real thing. These creamy confections look great tied with a colorful ribbon.

4 cups milk coatings

1 fudge bar mold

12 popsicle sticks

12 two inch cello bags

and ribbon (optional)

Melt the milk coatings as on page 20. Fill each fudge bar cavity with milk coatings. Be careful not to overfill the favor cavity. Tap the mold gently on the counter. Place a popsicle stick into each fudge bar making sure the stick is at least one inch into the coatings. Refrigerate 15 to 20 minutes until the fudge bars release easily from mold. Repeat with milk coatings until you have the desired number of favors. Let come to room temperature before you package with a cello bag and ribbon.

Ice Cream Swirl

Makes 12 swirls

Reminiscent of a traditional ice cream swirl. But this one is all confection.

3 cups milk coatings	3 cups light green coatings
2 cup white coatings	1 ice cream swirl mold
3 cups pink coatings	12 six inch paper sticks
3 cups yellow coatings	12 two inch cello bags and ribbon

Place 1 cup milk coatings and 2 cups white coatings together in a large microwave safe bowl. Melt in microwave on 50% power for 30 seconds. Stir. Repeat until melted. Stir until both colors are completely mixed and you have a tan color. Using a medium skewer as a paint brush, apply the tan coatings to your brush and paint the cone on all four of the ice creams in the mold, applying more coatings when needed. Let dry.

Melt the rest of the milk coatings as on page 20. When the cones are completely dry fill each favor cavity with milk coatings. Be careful not to overfill favor cavity. Tap the mold gently on the counter. Place a sin inch paper stick into each favor making sure the stick is at least one inch into the coatings. Refrigerate 15 to 20 minutes until the favors release easily from the mold. Repeat using different colors of coatings until you have the desired number of favors. Let come to room temperature before you package with a cello bag and ribbon.

Sonia's Tips: The tips of the swirl have a tendency to break off when your unmolding them. Pull up and forward holding the paper stick.

Orange Creamsicles

Makes 12 sicles

I remember these as a kid. Creamy and delicious. These are vanilla flavored coatings but also creamy and delicious. I show them here in assorted colors, but all orange is traditional.

1 cup orange coatings	1 orange creamsicle mold
4 cups white coatings	12 popsicle sticks
1 cup pink coatings	12 two inch cello bags and ribbon
1 cup yellow coatings	

Melt the orange coatings in a small microwave safe bowl on 50% power for 30 seconds. Stir. Repeat until melted. Using a small spoon apply the orange coatings into the cavity and going up the sides on all four of the ice creams in the mold. (For this step you are coating the mold cavity for the color effect, not pouring). Applying more coatings when needed. Let dry.

Melt the white coatings as on page 20. When the orange coatings are completely dry fill each cavity with white coatings. Be careful not to overfill the cavity. Tap the mold gently on the counter. Place a popsicle stick into each favor making sure the stick is at least one inch into the coatings. Refrigerate 15 to 20 minutes until favors release easily from mold. Repeat using different colors of coatings until you have the desired number of favors. Let come to room temperature before you package with a cello bag and ribbon.

3-D Lighthouse

Makes 1 lighthouse

You will spend most of your time trying to convince people you made this. This is a wonderful mold with a lot of detail. So much detail you have the option of painting the door with white coatings and the port holes with dark coatings or skipping that part and pouring it plain. Which ever you choose the finished piece will be impressive.

1/4 cup dark coatings	1 lighthouse mold
1 cup milk coatings	1 four inch cello bag
2 cups white coatings	ribbon

Melt the dark coatings in a small custard bowl in the microwave on 50% power for 30 seconds. Stir. Repeat until completely melted. Using a medium skewer as a paint brush, apply the dark coatings to your brush and paint the door and port holes. Being carefully to keep the edges smooth. Applying more coatings when needed. Let dry.

Combine the milk coatings with the white coatings and melt as on page 20. Stir well until you have a tan color. Beginning with the back half of the lighthouse mold, pour enough coatings into it so it is 3/4 full. Set aside where it will not tip over. Holding the front half of the lighthouse, pour enough coatings into it so it is 1/4 full. Set aside where it will not tip over. Hold the back half of the lighthouse mold in your left hand keeping it level so no coatings drip out. Pick up the front half of the lighthouse in your right hand and quickly put the front half onto the back half. Be sure to align the edges. Apply the metal clips to all sides of the lighthouse. Once you have the clips in place and are sure the coatings will not drip out, roll the mold around gently so the coatings cover the entire insides of the lighthouse. Set in the refrigerator face down for 15 minutes.

Turn face up and refrigerate 15 to 20 more minutes. Turn once more to face down. Refrigerate 15 more minutes or until it has cooled enough to remove from mold.

When the mold feels cold to the touch, take it out of the refrigerator and remove the clips. Gently insert you finger between the molds and try lifting off the top. This should be very simple. If they do not easily come apart return to the refrigerator for 15 minutes and try to remove the molds again. Note: if your lighthouse will not stand up on its own, use a paring knife to level the bottom of the lighthouse.

Let come to room temperature before you package with a cello bag and ribbon.

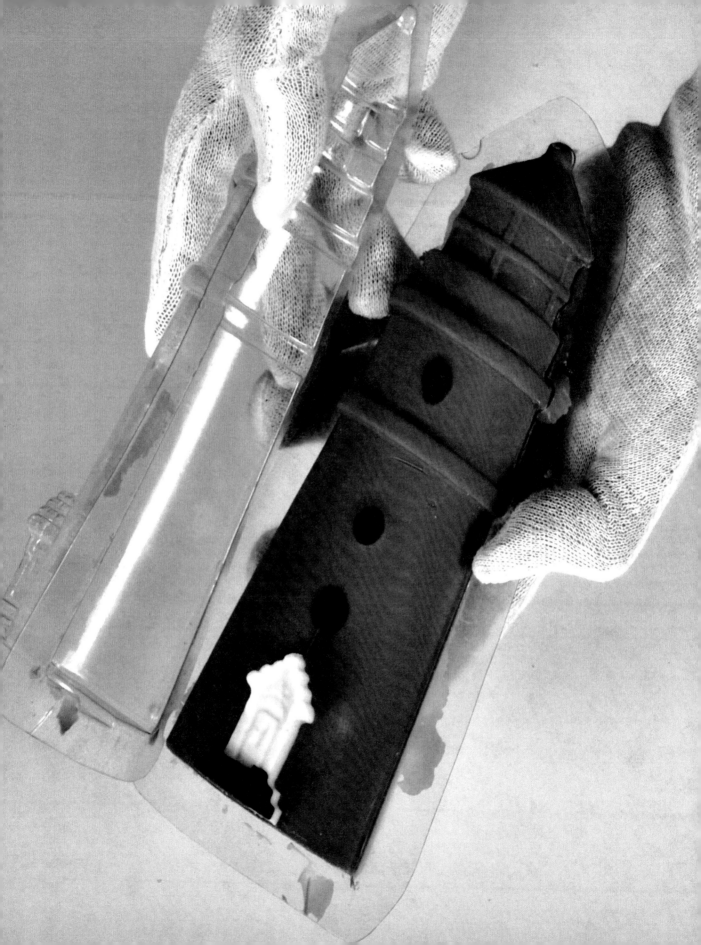

Lobsters and Crabs

Makes 8 lobsters and 8 crabs

Mixing red and white coatings in a swirl gives these sea creatures an authentic look. Try a blue ribbon to represent the ocean.

3 cups red coatings

1 cups white coatings

1/2 cup dark coatings

1 lobster favor mold

1 crab favor mold

16 four inch paper sticks

16 two inch cello bags and

ribbon (optional)

Place the red coatings and white coatings in separate microwave safe bowls. Melt in microwave as on page 20. Stir. Repeat until melted. Pour the white coatings into the red coatings and stir 5 times. The coatings will have a marble look to it. Using a spoon, fill lobster favors with the red coatings mixture. Be careful not to overfill the lobster cavity. Tap the mold gently on the counter. Place a four paper stick into each favor making sure the stick is at least one inch into the coatings. Refrigerate 15 to 20 minutes until lobsters release easily from mold. Repeat with the crab mold until you have the desired number of favors. Melt the dark coatings in the microwave on 50% power for 30 seconds. Stir. Repeat until melted. Using a medium skewer apply a dot of dark coatings to resemble the eyes. Let come to room temperature before you package with a cello bag and ribbon.

Starfish

Makes 12 starfish

It is fun to use different colors when making these starfish. They are big enough for party favors or omit the paper stick and they are small enough to put on a cake or cupcake.

2 cups milk coatings

2 cups yellow coatings

2 cups orange coatings

1 starfish mold

12 four inch paper sticks

12 two inch cello bags and

ribbon (optional)

Melt the milk, yellow and orange coatings in separate large bowls in the microwave on 50% power for 45 seconds. Stir. Repeat until melted. Fill each starfish cavity with milk coatings. Be careful not to overfill the cavity. Tap the mold gently on the counter. Place a four inch paper stick into each starfish making sure the stick is at least one inch into the coatings. Refrigerate 15 to 20 minutes until the starfish release easily from mold. Repeat with the assorted colors of coatings until you have the desired number of favors. Let come to room temperature before you package with a cello bag and ribbon.

Conch Shells

Makes 6 shells

If I did not know better I would think these conch shells came right out of the Pacific Ocean. Try marbling your coatings and making multi colored shells.

3 cups pink coatings

3 cups milk coatings

3 cups red coatings

1 conch shell mold

14 metal clips

6 four inch cello bags and

ribbon (optional)

Melt the pink coatings in the microwave on 50% power for 60 seconds. Stir. Repeat until melted. Beginning with the back half of the shell mold, pour enough coatings into it so it is 3/4 full. Set aside where it will not tip over. Holding the front half of the shell, pour enough coatings into it so it is 1/2 full. Set aside where it will not tip over. Hold the back half of the shell mold in your left hand. Pick up the front half of the shell in your right and quickly put the front half onto the bottom half. Be sure to align the edges. Apply the metal clips to all sides of the shell. Once you have the clips in place and are sure the coatings will not drip out, roll the mold around gently so the coatings cover the entire insides of the shell. You may need to tap the shell gently on the counter to force the coatings into the narrow part of the mold. Set in the refrigerator for 15 minutes.

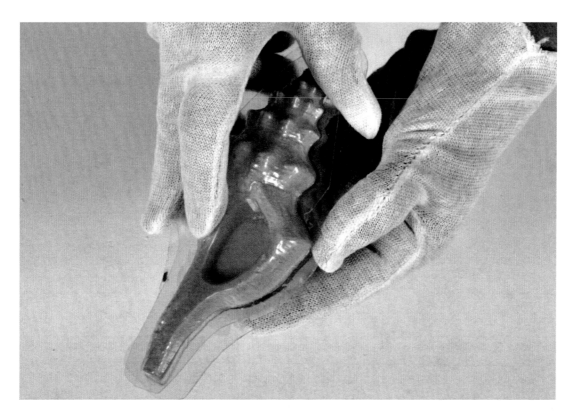

Turn over and refrigerate 15 more minutes. Turn once more. Refrigerate 10 more minutes or until it has cooled enough to remove from mold.

When the mold feels cold to the touch, take it out of the refrigerator and remove the clips. Gently insert your fingers between the molds and try lifting off the top. This should be very simple. If they do not come apart easily return to the refrigerator for 15 minutes and try to remove the molds again. Repeat using different colors of coatings until you have the desired number of shells. Let come to room temperature before you package with a cello bag and ribbon.

Confection Flip Flops

Makes 12 flip flops

So many people from every walk of life wear flip flops. My kids wear them year around. This style is especially cute and delicious.

1/2 cup pink coatings	1 flip flop mold
1/2 cup orange coatings	12 four inch paper sticks
1/2 cup yellow coatings	12 two inch cello bags and
2 cups milk coatings	ribbon (optional)
2 cups white coatings	

Place the 1/2 cup of pink, orange and yellow coatings in separate microwave safe bowls. Melt in microwave on 50% power for 30 seconds. Stir. Repeat until coating colors are melted. Keep colors on warming tray while you work. Using a medium skewer as a paint brush, apply the yellow coatings to your brush and paint the center of each flower on all of the four flip flops in the mold, applying more coatings when needed. Let dry. Using the same technique paint the flip flop straps with orange coatings and the flower with pink coatings. Let dry.

Melt the milk and white coatings as on page 20. When the colors in the mold are completely dry fill each Flip Flop cavity with milk coatings. Be careful not to overfill favor cavity. Tap the mold gently on the counter. Place a four paper stick into each favor making sure the stick is at least one inch into the coatings. Refrigerate 15 to 20 minutes until favors release easily from mold. Repeat using different colors of coatings until you have the desired number of favors. Let come to room temperature before you package with a cello bag and ribbon.

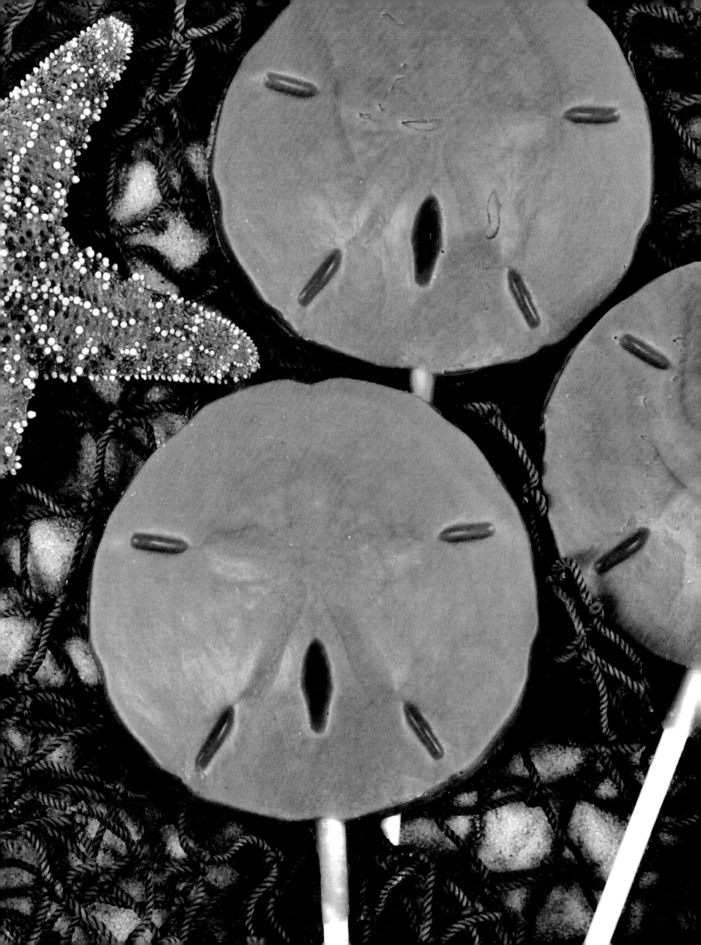

Sand Dollars

These sand dollars pair up great with the others shells in this chapter. Try using an aqua blue ribbon on them to represent the ocean.

2 cups milk coatings

3 cups white coatings

1 sand dollar mold

12 four inch paper stick

12 three inch cello bags and

ribbon (optional)

Place the milk coatings and the white coatings together in a large microwave safe bowl. Melt in microwave as on page 20. Stir until you have a tan color. Using a spoon, fill the sand dollar favors with the tan coating mixture. Be careful not to overfill the sand dollar cavity. Tap the mold gently on the counter. Place a four inch paper stick into each favor making sure the stick is at least one inch into the coatings. Refrigerate 15 to 20 minutes until sand dollars release easily from mold. Repeat until you have the desired number of favors. Let come to room temperature before you package with a cello bag and ribbon.

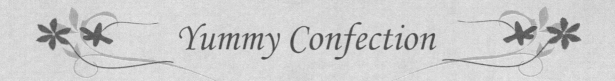

Yummy Confection

When it comes down to dipping, I see no reason for limits. Anything can be dipped in compound coatings. If you can eat it, you might try to dip it. I recommend the dipped potato chips. People are always surprised at how yummy they are.

Dipped Strawberries	150
Dipped Mellows	152
Dipped Sandwich Cookies	155
Spoons	157
Mini Cupcakes	159
Dipped Pretzels	163
Dipped Potato Chips	165

6

Dips and Treats

Dipped Strawberries

Makes 12 strawberries

Our most requested item. Dipped strawberries are a favorite of young and old. Use your imagination with these strawberries and create your own family favorite. Chopped nuts, sprinkles, mini chocolate chips, whatever you like.

4 cups milk coatings	12 large strawberries
1 cup white coatings	chopped nuts (optional)
1 cup dark coatings	sprinkles (optional)

Cover a cookie sheet with wax or parchment paper.   Melt the milk, white and dark coatings in separate bowls as directed on Page 20. Use a tall microwave safe container if possible for the milk coatings. Holding the strawberry by the leaves, dip each strawberry one at a time allowing the excess coatings to drip back into the bowl. Place the strawberries on the prepared cookie sheet. To drizzle with white or dark coatings, dip a fork into the white coatings, drizzle over the strawberries with a back and fourth motion. Or sprinkle with your favorite topping. Cool in the refrigerator 10 minutes. Repeat until you have the desired number of strawberries. Serve immediately.

Sonia's Tips: Strawberries should be rinsed with water and towel dried before dipping. I do not recommend refrigeration. Dip, cool, and serve for best results.

Dipped Mellows

Makes 18 mellows

Dipped marshmallows make great party favors and work well in treat bags. Try serving them with a batch of brownies or cookies for a new twist.

3 cups milk coatings   20 marshmallows

2 cups dark coatings   assorted sprinkle and nuts (optional)

Cover a cookie sheet with wax or parchment paper. Melt milk and dark coatings in separate large bowls as directed on Page 20. Use tall microwave safe containers if possible. Drop one marshmallow into the melted coatings. Using a dipping fork, push the marshmallow down into coatings to completely cover the marshmallow. Use the dipping fork to lift the marshmallow out of the coatings. Hold the marshmallow over the bowl allowing the extra coatings to drip back into the bowl. Place marshmallow on the prepared cookie sheet. Decorate by drizzling with dark coatings or sprinkling with rainbow sprinkles. Cool in the refrigerator 10 minutes. Repeat using different flavor combinations until you have the desired amount of mellows. Store in an air tight container.

Sonia's Tips: To drizzle with dark coatings dip a fork into the dark coatings and drizzle over the marshmallow with a back and fourth motion.

Dipped Sandwich Cookies

Makes 14 cookies

The first time I saw a dipped cookie was twenty years ago when a friend brought one home from Los Angeles. She had no idea what it was but loved it. I use these dipped cookies in many of our three dimensional confections, like the Teacup and Saucer found on page 60. They may be used for any occasion by simply changing the decoration.

4 cups milk coatings	14 sandwich cookies
1/2 cup white coatings	14 assorted royal icing shapes

Cover a cookie sheet with wax or parchment paper. Set aside. Melt milk and white coatings in separate bowls as directed on Page 20. Use a tall microwave safe container for the milk coatings if possible. Drop cookies into the milk coatings one at a time. Using a dipping fork push the cookie down into coatings to completely cover the cookie. Use the dipping fork to lift the cookie out of the coatings. Hold the cookie over the bowl, allowing the extra coatings to drip back into the bowl. Place cookies on the prepared cookie sheet. Decorate by drizzling with white coatings, sprinkling with rainbow sprinkles, or applying the royal icing shapes. Cool in the refrigerator 10 minutes. Repeat until you have the desired number of cookies. Store in an air tight container.

Note: To drizzle with white coatings, dip a fork into the white coatings and drizzle over the cookie with a back and forth motion.

Confection Spoons

Makes 15 spoons

These spoons are great with coffee, hot chocolate or as a beautiful snack. Serve with a hot beverage on Mother's Day, at Baby Showers, Wedding Receptions, or any special occasion. To enjoy the flavor at its very best, stir the spoon in the hot beverage then lick the confection as it is melting.

3 cups milk coatings	1 spoon mold
15 gold spoon sticks	15 - 2x10" flat cello bags (optional)
15 royal icing flowers or	15 twelve inch ribbon (optional)
holiday royal icings	

Melt the milk coatings as on page 20. Fill the spoon cavity's with coatings. Place a spoon stick into each spoon cavity. Tap the mold gently on the table to remove air bubbles and smooth the tops of the spoons. Place a royal icing shape in the middle of the spoon. Refrigerate 10 to 15 minutes until spoons release from mold easily. Repeat until you have the desired number of spoons. If desired, placed in a cello bag and tied with a beautiful ribbon.

Spoons can also be made with white coatings or dark coatings.

Colored coatings may be perfect for accenting your event theme. Below are a few combinations that you may like.

White spoons with a royal icing flag for Independence Day.

Pale pink spoons with a royal icing butterfly for a little girl party.

Dark spoon with a royal icing football for the big game.

Milk spoons with a royal icing bunny or carrot for Easter.

Light blue with a royal icing sea creature for summer.

Light brown spoon with a royal icing sea shell for a beach bon fire.

Mini Cupcakes
Filled with Peanut Butter

Makes 20 mini cupcakes

I am sure you will think of many occasions to offer these, over the top cute, mini cupcakes. Purchased mini peanut butter cups make this recipe quick and simple.

1 cup white coatings
1 cup yellow coatings
1 cup pink coatings
1 cup milk coatings
1 cup non pariels, multi color

20 mini peanut butter cups.
1 mini cupcake mold
20 two inch cello bags (optional)
ribbon (optional)

Melt the white coatings in microwave on 50% power for 30 seconds. Stir. Repeat until melted. Fill desired number of cupcake tops with white coatings. Tap gently on the counter to smooth tops and release air bubbles.

Refrigerate 10 to 15 minutes until tops release easily from mold. Repeat with remaining coating colors until you have the desired number of tops. Arrange the cupcake tops on a cookie sheet.

Place same number of mini peanut butter cups on the cookie sheet. Place a small amount of coatings, the same color as your top, onto the mini peanut butter cup. Place the cupcake top onto the mini peanut butter cup. Center the top and press down lightly. Repeat with all bottoms and tops. Refrigerate 5 minutes.

Using a skewer as your paint brush, start at the top of the cupcake and apply a thin line of coatings the same color as the top in a circular design. Less is better here. Dip the cupcake top into the non pariels. Let dry on the cookie sheet 10 minutes. Store in an air tight container or decorate with a cello bag and ribbon.

Dipped Pretzels

Dipped pretzels are a favorite at Chocolates By Imagination. Not only do our customers love to eat them, our staff loves to make them. Try packaging them in cello bags with a pretty ribbon instead of cookies and fudge.

3 cups milk coatings

3 cups dark coatings

20 classic style pretzels

1/2 cup white coatings

1/2 rainbow sprinkles

4 inch cello bags (optional)

ribbon (optional)

Cover a cookie sheet with wax or parchment paper. Melt the milk and dark coatings in separate large bowls as directed on page 20. Use a tall microwave safe container if possible. One at a time, drop a pretzel into melted coatings. Using a dipping fork push the pretzel down into coatings to completely cover the pretzel. Use the dipping fork to lift the pretzel out of the coatings. Hold the pretzel over the bowl allowing the extra coatings to drip back into the bowl. Place the pretzels on the prepared cookie sheet. Decorate them by drizzling with white coatings or sprinkling with rainbow sprinkles. Cool in the refrigerator 10 minutes. Repeat until you have the desired number of pretzels. Store in an air tight container.

Dipped Potato Chips

Makes 40 chips

Sound a little strange? That is the usual response. But then they try one and they are hooked. The crunch, the creamy chocolate flavor, the sweet and salty. Yummy! These dipped chips can be dipped in your favorite flavor. Try filling a pretty cello bag with them and surprising a friend or co-worker. I think you will be surprised by the response. Great for holiday treat bags too.

3 cups milk coatings

3 cups dark coatings

1 ten ounce bag potato chips
with ridges

4 inch cello bags (optional)

ribbon (optional)

Cover a cookie sheet with wax or parchment paper. Melt the milk and dark coatings in separate bowls as directed on Page 20. Use a tall microwave safe container if possible. Dip each chip one at a time allowing the excess coatings to drip back into the bowl. Place the chips on the prepared cookie sheet. When the cookie sheet is full, cool in the refrigerator 10 minutes. Repeat until you have the desired number of chips. Store in an air tight container or put in cello bags and decorate with ribbon.

Conversion Table

Weight to Measurements conversion table for

chocolate flavored buttons

Solid Chocolate Buttons	*Solid Chocolate Buttons*
1.5 ounces	¼ cup
3 ounces	½ cup
6 ounces	1 cup
12 ounces	2 cups
½ pound	1 ¼ cup
1 pound	2 ½ cups
1 ½ pounds	3 ¾ cups
2 pounds	5 cups
2 ½ pounds	6 ¼ cup
3 pounds	7 ½ cups
3 ½ pounds	8 ¾ cup
4 pounds	10 cups

Conversion Table

Weight to liquid conversion table for

chocolate flavored buttons

Solid Chocolate Buttons	Melted Chocolate Buttons
8 ounces	¾ cup
1 pound	1 2/3 cups
1 ½ pound	2 1/3 cups
2 pounds	3 ¼ cups
2 ½ pounds	4 cups
3 pounds	4 ¾ cups
3 ½ pounds	5 ½ cups
4 pounds	6 ¼ cups
4 ½ pounds	7 cups
5 pounds	7 ¾ cup
5 ½ pounds	8 ½ cups
6 pounds	9 ¼ cups

Melted measurements are rounded down to accommodate conventional measuring cups.

Source

Chocolates By Imagination

Glendora, Ca 91741

www.chocolatesbyimagination.com

As you thumb through the pages of this book, I hope you will see many new ideas you want to share with your family and friends. Every confection in this book is tried and true. I have made each one of these hundreds of times. They are the confections I most enjoy sharing with my family, friends, and customers.

Sonia